THE ULTIMATE
color
printer
CRAFT BOOK

THE ULTIMATE color printer

CRAFT BOOK

SUSAN KRZYWICKI
LAUREL BURDEN

WATSON-GUPTILL PUBLICATIONS / NEW YORK

Senior Editors: Candace Raney and Joy Aquilino
Edited by Amy Handy
Designed by pink design, inc. (www.pinkdesigninc.com)
Graphic production by Ellen Greene
Photography by Scott Smith of Smith/Nelson

First published in 2001 by Watson-Guptill Publications,
a division of BPI Communications, Inc.,
770 Broadway, New York, N.Y. 10003.
Visit us on the Web at http://www.watsonguptill.com/

Library of Congress Cataloging-in-Publication Data
Krzywicki, Susan.
    The ultimate color printer craft book / Susan Krzywicki, Laurel Burden.
        p. cm.
    Includes index.
    ISBN 0-8230-0750-2
    1. Paper work. 2. Color computer printers. I. Burden, Laurel, 1946– II. Title.
    TT870.K69 2001
    745.54—dc21
                2001026371

Manufactured in Malaysia

First printing, 2001

1 2 3 4 5 6 7 8 9 / 09 08 07 06 05 04 03 02 01

Dedication

We dedicate this book to our family and friends.

This book is in memory of my father. —**SUSAN E. KRZYWICKI**

For my mom, who knew my potential, and my father, who believed in me
to the end. —**LAUREL BURDEN**

Acknowledgments

Thanks to the Hewlett-Packard Company for providing us with technical and
marketing support to present this book. Numerous individuals over a two-year
period were available to discuss techniques, resources, and tech specs. Their
products stand for excellence and we are proud to have had the opportunity to
work with them.

We would also like to applaud the folks at Watson-Guptill, especially Joy
Aquilino and Amy Handy, who hung in there with us to ensure accuracy of detail
and consistency of approach. Candace Raney, senior editor, and Sharon Kaplan,
managing editor, steered us through the complex shoals of creating a book about
this pioneering field.

Laurel wishes particularly to thank Bobby and Patti for the many years of
support and love that keep her going, and Amy, Chris, Riki, Tim, and Carl, who
helped her in countless ways.

Susan thanks Kathy, Windy, Janet, and her sister, Tara. They all gave laughter,
ideas, and encouragement.

The Hobby Industry Association's annual convention gave us a great opportunity to meet a variety of helpful people, to learn about new techniques and products, and to network with folks from all over the globe. We thank them for
consistently offering such a strong marketing forum to people like us. We'd also
like to thank the many crafters around the United States who came to our
classes, talked to us online, and tried out the projects. The marriage of technology and art is in its infancy and a number of people from both worlds were
involved. We'd like to acknowledge these unnamed folks for their information
and generosity as we groped our way along. Using these new tools in unexpected
ways involves a good deal of serendipity and experimentation. We congratulate
those who try the unknown and take personal risks to create.

CONTENTS

Resolution issues, page 13

Postcards, page 41

Halloween Mask, page 74

Paper Airplane, page 78

Memory Quilt, page 103

Desk Accessories, page 117

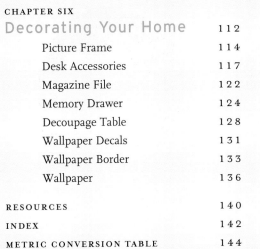

INTRODUCTION

If you're like most computer owners, you probably have a sneaking suspicion that you're not using your equipment to its fullest potential. If you're a crafter with a color printer on your desktop, you're probably right! Color printers are the most exciting development since color displays came to the home market. The advent of inexpensive color printers opens up a world of opportunities and ideas for all of us, from beginner to power user. There is so much you can do with a computer, some simple software, and a color printer—the ultimate craft tool.

This book will get you started on the creative process of using a color printer for fun at home. We demonstrate ideas you can share with your family, business associates, fellow crafters, and friends. Whip up projects to delight loved ones with a colorful expression of your creativity. Brighten up your home or office. Learn to print on fabric and other unusual materials. Enhance your computer skills with some interesting new techniques.

These projects are meant to be inspirations and tools to help you explore. Some of the ideas are very easy to make, some require additional materials, others take more time, and some are great new workings of old ideas. But all of them are *fun*.

We begin with "The Creative Desktop," an overview of hardware, software, and craft materials. Here you'll find general advice on color printers, definitions of key terms, and a roundup of helpful supplies. Following this introductory chapter, the projects are divided into five sections:

PAPER PROJECTS

HOLIDAY AND GIFT IDEAS

TOYS AND GAMES

FABRIC PROJECTS

DECORATING YOUR HOME

Start either with a simple project that catches your eye or with a specific goal in mind, such as a gift for someone or a set of items for an upcoming party. Change and adapt the projects as you work through them; you're sure to have your own great ideas that can be realized through the magic of a color printer.

Paper is just the beginning. Think of all the surfaces that paper can be attached to: fabric, wood, ceramic, glass, plastic, and many more. You'll also discover how to print on nonpaper surfaces, which will expand your options tremendously.

We start by covering some fundamentals for using color printers—no matter what the make or model of your equipment—and we show you what features to look for if you are in the market for something new. We've included a list of basic crafting materials used throughout the book and a section on the computer techniques that you will need to know. Then comes the heart of the book, the step-by-step projects. Each set of instructions includes a key specifying all the materials and tools you'll need, the type of software that is most useful for the applicable techniques, the general skill level required, and the approximate completion time. Finally, the appendix details sources for materials and supplies.

Let's get started! It is a rich and exciting world—time to try something new. Begin with something really easy like the pretty bookmark or the cool paper airplanes, or just flip through the book till something catches your eye.

Susan E. Krzywicki and Laurel Burden

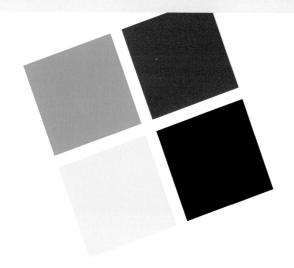

100%

80%

60%

CHAPTER ONE

the creative desktop

INK-JET PRINTER BASICS

Ink-jet printers spray very tiny drops of ink on a page in a tight pattern to create an image. Color printers do this using a combination of three primary colors: cyan (a very pure blue), magenta (somewhat like a red with strong purple undertones), and yellow, sometimes adding black as a fourth color. Believe it or not, these three colors are the only ones your printer needs to create a range of 16 million tones.

All the projects in this book can be accomplished on any type of color printer, although for home use, ink-jet printers are the most common. The technology in every brand of ink-jet printer is fairly similar, with variations in these areas:

1 **Speeds and feeds** The speed at which a printer operates will not affect the quality of your printing, but it does factor into your working methods. When beginning a project, a bit of advance planning can alleviate frustration with a slower printer.

2 **Image clarity** Image clarity is affected both by your printer's resolution capabilities (how many dots per inch it will print) and by the paper you choose. Greater resolution and better paper will yield a higher-quality image.

3 **Ease of installation and ongoing use** Fortunately, all printers now offer fairly simple installation, though various models may call for slightly different setups. The ease and frequency of changing toner cartridges is another factor to consider.

Speeds and Feeds

The speed of a printer doesn't affect quality (except with some printers in draft mode), but it can make a big difference in how satisfied you are with the overall results. Speed is measured in pages per minute. Generally, printers are slower in color mode than in black-and-white mode. The range for color printing may be from two pages per minute up to about ten pages per minute. Manufacturers define color printing as a full page with some text, a logo, or images on the page.

Note that "photographic prints," "prints," and "photos" refer to a full page of intense, overall color with continuous tones. Continuous tones are what you see when you look at a picture in a magazine or at a photograph from a film-processing company. The complexity required to process the information streaming from the computer and to spray that much ink on a page makes a dramatic difference in speed. Current models are rated at two to three minutes per page for full-page photographic prints.

To decide how print speed will affect you, consider your needs. For example, if you plan to make dozens of photo-graphic prints, a printer that turns out a color image once every three minutes is likely to leave you pretty frustrated. But if, like many crafters, you work in bursts, in a step-by-step mode, you will probably find that your working pace is not slowed down by your printer. Often, by planning ahead, you can batch your printing and alleviate the potential bottleneck. Print your homemade Christmas cards in late November while you work on other tasks, keeping an eye out for chores like refilling the paper tray and watching for jams.

Experiment with your software to determine what types of images take a long time to print and plan accordingly. Time how long it takes to print full-page color images, then make a note of the timings on the printouts and include these in your sample book. (See pages 22–23 for information on creating a sample book.)

Image Clarity

The subject of image clarity encompasses two similar acronyms, dpi and ppi. There is often some confusion about them (some software products even use them interchangeably), but they actually pertain to different yet related concepts. **Dpi** (dots per inch) refers to the resolution of the printer—how many drops of ink it lines up in a row to make the images. The printer that concentrates more dots per inch produces a higher-quality image, up to a certain point. **Ppi** (pixels per inch), on the other hand, is a measurement of how many bits of light are available in a row on a monitor. The resolution of the image itself may be any number, depending on the resolution at which it was scanned. The monitor's inherent capability will enable it to display only so many ppi (generally 72 ppi).

To make matters more confusing, you may be printing a 300-ppi image on printer that can see only 150 ppi, even though it has a 700-dpi resolution. This is because the internal processing engine of the printer has a finite amount of memory in which to translate computer language into printer instructions. The printer interpolates the image information and takes time to drop data that it cannot use by down-sampling. Because the printer has to drop all this extra data, it may slow your print job. The key to this whole discussion is to scan your images based on what their final use will be. If the image is only for on-screen use, 72 ppi is fine. For printed matter, test your image at around 150 ppi. Resolution settings any higher than that may simply be wasting both disk space and processing time.

Any printer resolution over 300 dpi is sufficient to make these projects look good and 700 dpi and above is great. Some printers offer different print resolutions, depending on your media and your desire for final print or a draft copy. Draft modes save ink and can be useful for testing layouts. Because they do not yield accurate color, they

The higher the resolution, the clearer the image. The section printed at 100 dpi looks blurry; at 300 dpi the image is clear and sharp.

are less useful for testing if color matching is important. Some printers are designed to offer higher resolutions in black-and-white mode, so check your specifications in the user's manual.

The current crop of printers includes models aimed at photo-quality images as opposed to text printing. This is an important distinction. (See the section on buying a new printer , pages 15–17, for more information about available options.)

The paper or other media on which you print will make a difference in output quality, color, and crispness. (See "Paper Choices" and "Other Media," pages 21–22, for information on this.) Lots of fun and interesting new choices are now on the market—check out the array of surfaces, finishes, colors, textures, and weights of paper, plastics, and fabrics that can be printed on. Do a little exploring and develop a collection for experimentation.

Ease of Installation and Ongoing Use

Luckily for the home user, all printers are now easy to install. The Macintosh still has a slight edge over the Wintel machines. (This term, from a combination of "Windows" and "Intel," refers to any machine, regardless of brand, that runs a Windows operating system and contains Intel computer chips.) The printer industry has emphasized "plug and play," meaning that manufacturers are becoming increasingly sophisticated in how they mask the setup complexity. Nowadays, to install most printers you simply plug in the cable and power cords, load a CD-ROM, and double-click on an installer program—that's all.

The software loads "drivers" for your printer and puts these small pieces of software in the right place on your hard drive. The software program you are working with can then hand over the printing tasks to the driver. You can be assured that your computer will maximize the differences in your brand of printer and use the highest resolutions, color settings, and print speeds. Drivers occasionally need to be updated, usually when you move to a new level of operating system. Generally, the process of installing the new operating system takes care of this task for you automatically, but every once in a while there may be problems. If your normally reliable printer causes trouble after a major upgrade, this could be the issue. (See "Troubleshooting," page 20, for more information.)

What You Need to Know About Toner

Changing the ink is another major consideration: how often do you need to do it and how simple is it to accomplish? Most current brands allow you to change the black cartridge separately from the colored inks, which makes sense since this is the well that runs dry most frequently. In the more sophisticated models, each color may be purchased separately.

Recently manufacturers have been adding features to warn you when a cartridge or a color is running low, so you can plan ahead when to change inks. Imagine spending almost three minutes printing a photo on expensive, high-quality paper, only to have one color run out in the last

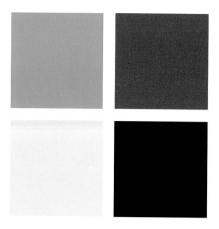

With just four colors—cyan (a very pure blue), magenta, yellow, and black—color printers can produce an astounding 16 million tones.

inch! With this new feature you can change the ink before-hand and save yourself time and frustration, not to mention the cost of paper and ink. The mechanisms used to determine when you will run out of ink vary. Some are optical sensors; some are calculations based on the type of printing. Keep your printer user's manual, since the ritual of changing inks may not be intuitively obvious. Store unused cartridges in a cool, dry place and watch the expiration dates. Old inks will clog and give poor results.

All current models of printers have a separate black ink reservoir. Some brands offer two black cartridges, which allows higher print speeds in black print mode, up to ten pages per minute. If you are using an older model, the printer needs to mix cyan, magenta, and yellow to make black. "Composite black" refers to color created by this

Here are a few other considerations, based on our experience of having tried just about everything at least once.

• DON'T open the ink cartridges. We have, and the ink was a big mess because it was so concentrated. It seemed to get all over everything before we knew what hit us, and it was not easy to clean up.

• At the beginning, we kept a piece of scrap paper nearby and made a hash mark for every color page we printed. This is an inexact calculation, but it at least gave us some insight into what we might expect over time. After two or three cartridges, we had some rough ideas.

mixing. A composite black is slightly less rich, takes a little longer to print, and uses slightly more ink. Read your instruction manual to determine how black tones are created. You may want to make samples of the different tones of black for future reference.

Occasionally the ink reservoirs may need to be cleaned and each printer has a different set of instructions for this. We have found that we clean the cartridges once every couple of months. Self-test directions are also included in your manual. Running these tests can help you determine which color or what alignment tracker is causing problems. Your manual will also give you very specific instructions on how to alleviate any of these problems.

In the section below on creating a sample book (page 22), we suggest that you may want to keep track of how often you run out of ink, and what color you use most frequently. Color ink-jet printer cartridges are not very inexpensive and they have expiration dates. Plan ahead so that you can price-shop and make the best deal possible. Of course, you will want to have a fresh supply of ink on hand so that you don't run out in the middle of a big project. We always purchase a new spare cartridge as soon as the current spare is in use.

Start early to price-shop for replacement cartridges. Look in our resource section (pages 140–41) for ideas on where to buy supplies. There may be as much as a 20 to 30 percent difference in the cost of the inks. Because the inks have expiration dates, be careful not to buy too far ahead of need, but do make note of good sources and availability or delivery times.

BUYING A PRINTER

The fast-paced world of technology is constantly offering new models, products, and features. Prices continue to fall or stay relatively stable but with each new generation of products you get more functionality for your money. You could drive yourself nuts waiting for the best deal or the right time to buy. The best deals are now and this *is* the right time to buy. So take courage in hand and follow these guidelines to find the right printer for you. The first step is to determine your specific printer needs by considering what kind of use you intend for your printer.

Evaluating Your Printer Needs

The type of material you will be printing most often is a major consideration when deciding on what type of printer will best suit your situation. Printer speed, image clarity, and ease of ongoing use all factor into this decision, so thought must be given to what sort of work you will be doing on the computer. Are you printing largely text-heavy documents, or are you mainly interested in high-quality visual images for use in various projects? The following user profiles will help you assess you printer needs.

User Profiles

There are three categories of home users. Which profile best describes your situation? Each of these scenarios will lead to slightly different choices.

1   You have a home-based business. You plan to print flyers, brochures, marketing materials, and customer-related documents. As your business grows, you may add employees. Think to the future and decide if you need to have a printer that will network easily. When you add a second computer, how will you give access to both users? There are a variety of networking schemes out there, from simple cable arrangements to full-blown home LANs (local area networks—sort of like home intercom systems for your PCs).

2   You work at home in the evenings on work you cannot complete in the office. You may print presentation materials or reports and proposals. Your family may want to use the printer for projects, homework, Internet research, crafts, and other fun stuff. You may still want to address networking issues if there are several computers scattered all over the house. Do you want one printer to serve the entire household or would it be better to buy a second color printer for the kids' use? Another concern is whether you need a printer aimed at printing photographs. A few models are sized and engineered specifically to print photo-sized images (around 4 x 6 inches) on special glossy paper.

3   You are a dedicated crafter and want to have free creative range to experiment on a variety of media. Your printer decision will have to be based on whether you need more of a photo printer or a color printer. Go for the fastest speed and the best resolution. Some of the newest printers have six colors for truer color fidelity, so check these out first. You'll need to see samples of the print quality, so your research path will require a little more hands-on time, and you may need to travel to see the actual printers in a variety of stores in order to satisfy your color sense. Then research the best source for purchasing. Be aware, though, that so many variables affect color that no matter how much time you spend examining sample prints, your results may vary.

Once you have an idea of your printer objectives, you're ready to begin studying the specifics of various models and vendors to see which ones best fit your needs. The following sections provide a game plan.

Researching Brands, Models, and Prices

Start by familiarizing yourself with brand names, then move to the major distinguishing factors: how the manufacturers describe speed, quality, networking, or plug-and-play capabilities. Look for warranty information, which is generally fairly standard, but some manufacturers may offer longer warranties as an indication of their commitment to the customer and their justifiable belief in their own products.

How much would you like to spend? Advertised specials for color ink-jet printers can be found for as low as about $100. At the high end you can expect to spend around $500. Shop very carefully, since prices vary widely. You might see an occasional "deal" with incredibly low prices, like $50 for last week's model. These can be great buys if you have done your homework and have assured yourself that the printer being offered is adequate for your needs.

- The Internet is by far the best resource for researching printers. See the resources section (pages 140–41) for URLs (Universal Resource Locators, the addresses for Web sites) of some major manufacturers. Not only can you search the manufacturers' sites, but they may allow you to buy online. A number of reputable retailers offer every type of computer product. If you aren't familiar with the companies and their backgrounds, you can use them just for research. Many vendors started out in catalog sales, so they have some track record and reputation. The other benefit to searching on the Internet is that you can find expert information anytime of the day or night.
- If you subscribe to any computer magazines, flip to the back to find dozens of ads for mail-order and online

sources for buying equipment. If you don't subscribe, pick up a few at the local newsstand. *Family PC* is a good start, as are *PC World* and *MacWorld*.

- You'll often find free local computer newspapers at the grocery store or office supply store. These magazines are usually focused on your hometown, will showcase retailers nearby, and may have classified ads for buying and selling.

- Find out about any local user groups for your type of computer. There are usually groups for Wintel machines and Macs, and there may be more specialized groups for programs such as Photoshop. These are filled with enthusiasts who can give you great advice and pricing information.

- Mail-order catalogs often have "bundles," a marketing arrangement where a piece of popular (or maybe not-so-popular) software is bundled into the price. These often add value without costing the manufacturer too much. The software companies like it because it helps them bring in more users and higher sales volumes for their products. But make sure you are comparing apples to apples. Do you need the extra features bundled with the printer? If you have a choice, what is the price without the bundle? Is the software a "light" version of the complete product? Is it an outdated version?

- Daily and Sunday newspapers have computer ads for the major warehouse-type stores. If you aren't finding ads in the metro or front section, check out the other sections; in our city, for example, these ads are found in the sports section.

- General retailers such as Sears also carry ink-jet printers. Shop them for information, research, and convenience.

The upcoming focus for printer manufacturers will be in the cost of consumables, warning lights for low ink, separate inkwells for each color (so that if you use lots of blue and constantly run out of this color first, you don't have to throw away the other reservoirs of ink), and speed. The manufacturers are keenly aware of the speed issue, so expect to see more progress in this area. We are fast approaching the time when all color ink-jet printers will produce "photorealistic" images and further discussion of dots per inch will become irrelevant. So focus on the areas that will offer the most differentiation.

Researching Vendors

Following is a sample comparison spreadsheet to help you determine which criteria are most important to you. Gather your information and rank your findings. Once you have considered all of these points and determined which features are important to you, you should have a very clear picture of what you hope to buy. It is a big decision, so consider carefully and have fun doing the research.

Printer Evaluation Checklist

FEATURE	OVERALL IMPORTANCE	VENDOR #1	VENDOR #2	VENDOR #3
Popular brand name	*(mark this with an A, B, or C)*			
Price				
Dpi				
Cost of consumables				
Updated printer drivers included				
Sample paper selection included				
Installation CD-ROM included				
Installation process				
Ease of installation				
Ease of use				
Network capabilities				
Mac/Wintel compatible				
Draft mode				

FEATURE	OVERALL IMPORTANCE	VENDOR #1	VENDOR #2	VENDOR #3
Popular brand name	*(mark this with an A, B, or C)*			
Cables included				
Maximum size of paper				
Envelopes				
Continuous form paper				
Minimum size of paper				
Separate black inkwell				
Out-of-ink indicator				
Photorealistic images				
Paper tray capacity				
Number of paper trays				
Composite black or true black				
Size of box ("footprint")				
Flexibility of placement on desk				
Additional software included				
Easy-to-read user manual				
Fonts				
Pages per minute color				
Pages per minute black				
Minutes per page photo				
Specialty inks				
Variety of media handled				
Maximum paper weight				
Minimum paper weight				
Controls on the front and easy to reach				
Paper path (a short, straight one is more reliable and easier to clear in case of a jam)				
Warranty				
Personal experience				
Others' comments				
Multipurpose or single-purpose				

Vendor Comparisons

After you've begun focusing your search on one or two models, spend some time deciding where to buy. The type of company you buy from can have a big impact over the life of your printer. Saving a few dollars on the front end may involve some risk or may lead to inconvenience in the future. Theoretically, each type of retailer has advantages and disadvantages. Your own experience may give you a different perspective. Ask people you know for their advice. Do you know an enthusiast who is constantly buying, upgrading, and talking computers? Small business owners and people who frequently purchase computer equipment may also be very knowledgeable. Even young people may have significant expertise in purchasing printers, and they are generally very enthusiastic about sharing their views.

The following comparison table offers an overall perspective on the pluses and minuses of different sources for printers.

	PLUS	MINUS
Mail order	Price competitive. Special offers.	Mailing back a product in case of problems. Fly-by-night companies do exist.
Local computer store	Convenience: returns and service may be easier. Employees are sometimes very knowledgeable. You can see the model you want and run sample prints.	Employees may not be very knowledgeable. Selection may be limited.
Large retailer	Price competitive. Wide selection.	Employees may not know the products very well. Products may still have to be returned to the manufacturer for warranty repairs. Store may not provide out-of-warranty repairs.
Direct from the manufacturer	Knowledgeable staff. Latest models available.	Company may not offer consumer-oriented services.
Internet sources	Every manufacturer has information galore. Every vendor has round-the-clock shopping access.	Some people are still not comfortable using their credit card over the Internet. (Note: Some Web sites allow you to search for information and then call them on a toll-free number to place an order.)

Vendor Evaluation Checklist

Once your vendor research has narrowed your choices to two or three vendors, consider the following issues and weight their importance to your purchase.

Remember to find out if a vendor will allow you to bundle other business into the transaction to get a better price.

ISSUE	VENDOR #1 IMPORTANCE *(mark this with an A, B, or C)*	VENDOR #2	VENDOR #3
Reliability			
Warranty			
Return for repair			
After warranty expires			
Customer satisfied with past purchases			
Heard good things from others			
Price			
Delivery			
Taxes			
Cost of delivery			
Discounts			
Future purchase programs			
Ease of access			
Politeness			
Knowledge level			

Service Issues

Who will service your purchase during the warranty period and afterward? Check your options. Look in your local yellow pages under "Computers" for ads that mention your prospective brand. Call the company with the following questions:

- Do they work on your proposed brand?
- Do they do warranty repair for your brand?
- Will they handle out-of-warranty repairs?
- Is there a minimum repair fee?

- Is there an "estimate of trouble" fee?
- What is the minimum turnaround for repairs?
- What do they do if they cannot fix the problem?

If you live in a remote part of the country, take a few moments to discover what the warranty policy covers. Will you be able to take your printer back to a local retailer or mail it to the point of purchase or the manufacturer, or will you rely on a local business for repairs? Once the machine is out of warranty, your choices become even more variable. (See the box "Troubleshooting" for more advice on this area.)

Troubleshooting

Because printers are electromechanical devices with more moving parts than any other part of your system, they are the weakest link in your entire setup. And because paper is such a variable factor, the likelihood of having something go wrong is much higher with a printer than another part of your system. The reliability of printers is remarkable in the face of all of these variables. But what happens if your printer stops working?

- First, check the owner's manual and follow its troubleshooting tips. If that doesn't fix the problem and the printer is still under warranty, call the place where you bought it and follow their instructions.

- If the warranty has expired, try calling tech support. Check the Web site for the manufacturer and look for helpful hints.

- If all attempts at troubleshooting fail, try swapping out some of the components: paper, cables, and ink reservoirs.

- If none of these approaches solve the problem, consider taking the printer to a local repair shop for an estimate, which usually entails a small fee that can be applied to any repair bill that you authorize. The general rule is that anything other than small repairs are not worth performing. For example, if there is an error in any of the electronics, the printer can only be repaired at the factory and this will cost more than the printer is worth.

If You Already Own a Color Printer

With technology evolving so rapidly, your printer may seem like an ancient relic, but it may continue to serve you well, and may even have some unnoticed capabilities. It is also nice to know the limits of your particular model. Following are some suggestions for reviewing your equipment, and gathering information and examples of how your printer works. Perhaps it really is time to purchase a newer model, or perhaps your current one is still perfectly adequate for your needs. Here are some points to explore, and to consider in relation to your user profile:

Speed: What is the rated speed of your printer? Is it faster in black-and-white mode than in color mode? How long does it take to print a full-page color image? How long does it take to print a page of black text?

Quality: What is the dpi rating? Is there a draft mode? Are there quality settings in your software: Highest, Medium, and Draft? When you ask the program you are in to print, your setup may bring up a window with choices in it. What are the defaults? What changes can you make to those settings?

Features: Does your printer allow you to use continuous form paper (very useful for making long banners), print on envelopes, load more than one envelope at a time, load 9-inch-wide paper, or use special inks like fluorescent colors? How much paper can you load in the paper tray? Are there two separate paper trays?

If you have owned your printer for more than three years, that is a good stretch and the new products will look very enticing. You may have seen your needs change over time. Consider buying a new printer when you begin to feel frustrated with either the speed or the capabilities of your equipment. Because the products change so fast, there is never a bad time to buy a printer.

USING YOUR PRINTER

Set up your printer as soon as possible, since your warranty clock is ticking, but take time to do it right. First read the manuals, and any help files on the installation CD, which always contains the latest news and contact information in case of trouble. Open the box and lay out the paraphernalia, comparing it to the shipping list. If anything is missing, tell the store immediately. Be sure you have the right printer cables, drivers, and a selection of paper. And have enough extra ink on hand so you don't run out in the middle of a job. Plan ahead to ensure the best price. (See "What You Need to Know About Toner," pages 13–14.) Make some test samples: black-and-white printing, color printing, and photo printing. If everything is working, then it's time to have some fun!

Selecting Paper and Other Printing Surfaces

To get good results, focus on a very important element: paper. There are a myriad of papers and related media for different uses. Each manufacturer recommends certain quality levels and types of paper, depending on which printer you buy. But this is just a starting point. Your own experience will guide you to certain brands, weights, price points, and types of papers. Think about what paper you will use most often, and search for the most competitive price you can find on that type of paper.

The printer package probably contains a sampler kit of papers from the manufacturer, including information on how to reorder. Look for the manufacturer's toll-free number. Warehouse-type stores such as Office Depot and Staples generally sell supplies, usually stocked near the printers themselves. Most of these retailers also carry T-shirt transfers and fabric sheets. A wealth of companies offer supplies by mail and online. (See the resources section, pages 140–41.) Other good sources are magazines like *MacWorld* or *PC Week*. Note that companies may have more items than are listed in their printed catalog, so call and ask specifically for the product you want.

It helps to test each project on your equipment. Different printers can give different results, as can choice of media. To see for yourself, select a photographic image, add some text, and draw a few boxes in other colors. Print this on everyday paper and then on high-quality paper. Notice the difference in image clarity and color intensity. Small details and the smaller text characters will be visibly different. Another area to check is the amount of rippling in the two samples. Since the ink is water-based, there will be more rippling the more intense the colors get. Obviously, in more humid climates, this effect will be compounded. We have not found a consistent correlation between rippling and cost/quality of paper, so you may want to run your own tests and choose a brand you can count on over time.

Paper Choices

Try to keep a variety of papers on hand at all times. Plain bond paper is fine for many uses, but special projects will look better on the more expensive high-quality or coated stock. The highest-quality papers offer maximum reflection of the inks to enhance the brilliance of the image. The resource section (pages 140–41) lists mail order sources for specialty items used in some of the projects.

Examine the store samples of different types of paper and ask the sales help for their expertise. Also buy some quality ink-jet paper, which is usually a middle-ground quality and price level. This paper has a polished surface and a higher reflectivity index, so your image appears more brilliant. It will not produce the very highest-quality images but will suffice for many projects. Remember to include a wide range of printed samples in your sample book for future reference (see pages 22–23).

Plain bond paper comes in both letter and legal sizes. It's fine for projects that don't need the best-quality output.

High-resolution paper may be called by a variety of names, including photo-output paper, photo-quality paper, high-quality paper, or final output paper. Its special white clay coating reflects colors at maximum brilliancy. It is more expensive than plain bond, so use it only for the final print on the projects that require your highest-quality output.

Specialty papers offer almost unlimited choices, such as marbled, shiny, colored, or with preprinted borders. (See the resources section, pages 140–41, for suppliers.)

Envelopes, card stock, and cover-weight paper also come in an almost endless variety. Watch the thickness to ensure your printer can accurately draw the envelope through its paper path. Card stock is great for notecards, invitations, postcards, and decorative items like boxes.

Laser-perforated labels are sold at stationery and office supply stores. These sheets of heavy-weight paper are prescored to separate cleanly and easily after printing. You can use them for business cards, postcards, and other applications. Because they are prescored, you don't have to trim them with a paper cutter or utility knife—just print and separate! Chose these if you prefer ease of use and speed. They cost more than plain card stock but are less work.

Self-adhesive paper is sold in $8^1/_2$- x 11-inch sheets and works well for making badges and labels. We also use it in a variety of creative ways, such as cutting up an overall printed image into smaller pieces that are used as collage elements (see the Magazine File, page 122, and the Decoupage Table, page 128), or sticking a large printed motif onto a surface as a decorative element (see the Wallpaper Decals, page 131).

Self-adhesive labels are available in various types, colors, and sizes, either arranged on $8^1/_2$- x 11-inch sheets or individually cut. The sheets can be loaded in most printers. Check the manual for information or restrictions on handling label sheets and run some test prints. Some printers let you stack the label sheets in the paper bin or the envelope slot; others require you to feed them one at a time. Some labels are large enough to be loaded individually like envelopes. Some printers won't feed sheets of labels if one label has been removed from a full sheet, so plan your prints beforehand.

Other Media

Some projects require printable media other than paper. To render an image on fabric you can use T-shirt transfers, or print directly on specially prepared fabric. (See page 95 for more information.) The resource section (pages 140–41) lists suppliers for some of the specialty items.

T-shirt transfer papers consist of a backing sheet on which has been layered a coating of plastic that melts at low temperatures. The printed image is held on this coated surface until, with the heat of an iron, the plastic—and thus the image—is fused onto a receptive surface. Firmly woven white or very light-colored natural fabrics work best; polyester and other synthetics may melt under the iron's heat, although cotton-polyester blends are often okay. T-shirts (especially the Hanes Beefy T), cocktail napkins, ties, and scarves are all great places to use these transfers. T-shirt transfers can be found at computer and office supply stores. (See page 94 for more information on working with this medium.) Occasionally, odors may arise as the transfer is fused onto fabric, so always follow the manufacturer's instructions, and work in a well-ventilated area.

Canon fabric sheets load into your printer so you can print directly on fabric. (See the project on pages 103–6.)

Muslin, cotton, and silk in white or off-white can be used to make your own fabric sheets. (See the project on pages 107–11.) All-natural fibers seem to work best for fabric printing since they absorb the inks more evenly and yield stronger colors. Some natural-synthetic blends may work, but be sure to make some test prints on fabrics you're considering before you commit the time and energy of completing a project on a particular fabric blend.

Nonfusible interfacing, available at fabric stores, can be cut into 8½- x 11-inch sheets and loaded into the paper tray for printing. (See the project on pages 98–102.)

Printing on Both Sides of the Paper

Many printers allow you to print on both sides of the paper. Check your owner's manual for specifics. Some printers prompt you through this reloading process with an on-screen wizard; others may warn you against even attempting to print on both sides.

If your printer does have this capacity, familiarize yourself with it. First, determine whether the printable or the nonprinting side should be face up in the tray. Make a note in your manual for future reference. When you load the tray, analyze which side of the paper is the printable side. Always be sure the ink is thoroughly dry before reloading the paper, to prevent two problems: smudging as the page passes through the printer, and the potential for jamming if the paper is rippled. Run a trial print, then when the ink is dry, flip the paper and reload it. If you are loading more than one sheet, be sure the edges align.

Protecting Your Prints

Ink-jet print, by its very nature, is susceptible to water damage. If liquids are spilled on the image, it will bleed no matter how long ago it was printed. To protect your projects, you can laminate them, coat them with spray varnish, or enclose the image in a protective frame or envelope. Several vendors offer laminating machines that plastic-coat pieces of paper measuring up to 8 ½ x 11inches. (See the resources section, page 140, for one vendor; machines run about $200.) If you'd rather not invest in a laminating machine, try peel-and-press sheets of self-laminating film (sold at office supply stores), or even clear contact paper.

Creating a Sample Book

A sample book provides a wonderful reference about various paper types, color appearance, resolution, and other aspects of printer output that you can consult when beginning a project. We assembled a three-ring binder with as many samples and as much information as we could. Following are some guidelines on what to put in your book.

- **Color samples** from Adobe Illustrator, Macromedia Freehand, or other drawing or layout programs, such as AppleWorks, InDesign, SmartDraw Pro, or CorelDRAW. A native suite is usually bundled with the hardware; check with your retailer, or review your packaging materials. Make samples at different resolutions and on different media. We labeled each swatch with all the variables: ppi, color name, formula for color (CMYK or RGB), and if a tint was printed. If color exactness is crucial then you must test for differences, since what you see on the screen may not be exactly what you get on your printer. Create a document in your drawing program made up of 1-inch squares and fill each with a different color. Type the formula for the color or the name of the color below each one, and create a blend, from 100 percent to 10 percent, next to each. Print it on your best paper and compare the printed sample with your screen image. Refer to this document when checking screen color to recall how that color will print.

- **Before-printing checklist** to remind yourself of all the items you need to pay attention to before hitting the print button. We often found, for example, that we forgot to switch on "high-quality" modes or specify the right number of prints we wanted, thus wasting time and materials. So we put together a checklist to avoid the problem. Use our sample checklist to develop your own.

  _____ Quality mode

  _____ Speed mode

  _____ Number of prints

  _____ Paper orientation

  _____ Gradient check

  _____ Print to a file for later processing

  _____ Size of file (the larger the file, the slower the print)

- **Media samples** of printing on various papers, labels, fabric, and other surfaces. Mark the name, source, and approximate price on the samples and enclose them in plastic sleeves.

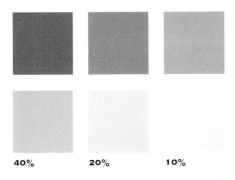

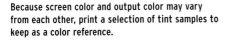

Because screen color and output color may vary from each other, print a selection of tint samples to keep as a color reference.

- **Examples of your work,** perhaps including a page of lines with rule width noted; textures; photos; typestyles at different resolutions; colors at varying resolutions and on different papers; a scanning resolution test; a screen resolution test; sample prints from favorite projects you may repeat; fabric you have printed on and washed, to see if the inks run or bleed; other fun samples you may have collected over the years. If you are new to scanners, the scanning resolution test is a very interesting learning experience. Scan a photo at a particular resolution, say 300 ppi. Save the scan and notice how much storage space it consumes. Scan the image again at a lower resolution, around 150 ppi, and save that. Scan the image again at around 72 ppi, and save. Finally, scan the image at around 10 ppi and save this final image. Note the difference in file sizes. Now print a copy of each at the highest resolution your printer can achieve. Note the differences. Open each of these images on your screen, and note which images are acceptably clear. Play around with sample ppi in the image and print copies of the two or three best images, documenting the resolution for future reference.

- **Articles or pictures from magazines** and notes from books or other sources that provide ideas, information, and inspiration. Keep in mind that although noncommercial use of other people's work is allowable within limits, you must respect the copyright laws for any projects that you plan to go public with. This means that you cannot scan another person's work and use it in a commercial endeavor without first gaining permission from the owner of the image. But our illustrations are copyright-free and for your use—scan them right out of this book if you wish.

Remember to test your ideas; it's often wise to make several samples. For example, we have found that some types of ink are unsuitable for certain media; transparency sheets and T-shirt transfers are particularly sensitive. Before creating a masterpiece with a medium like transfer paper, test the process on a small sample piece, from the initial printing all the way through washing and ironing. When in doubt, test it out.

Testing the Outer Limits

You may want to explore the possibilities of using your printer on media not indicated in the specifications for your model. Be careful, since any problems that arise may void your warranty or cause repair bills. In the years that we have been working with a variety of brands, models, and ages of printers, we have had some near-disasters, mostly involving paper jams. We once printed a beautiful floral design on very thin interfacing that wound itself around the feed mechanism and caused us some very tense moments.

If you are going to stretch the performance of your printer, make sure you take reasonable precautions. Plan ahead: most repair and customer-support organizations may not be available on weekends. Test one variable at a time. For example, try printing on a heavier weight of plain bond paper before you use a slippery, thick sheet of plastic. Inks generally dry fairly rapidly but we have had our share of smudged results, so be sure prints are thoroughly dry, especially if you have used deep tones or large areas of color or are printing on any nonpaper surfaces.

THE REST OF YOUR DESKTOP

Beginning computer skills are necessary to accomplish the projects in this book. If you have never used a computer before it will be helpful to take a class or have someone help you acquire the knowledge base in order to get started. We assume you know how to "point and click." If these terms are unfamiliar, please begin with your introductory user's manual.

We have included here a list of all of the major tools and techniques we refer to in the projects. When you read the directions for each venture and come across a term you do not understand, refer back to this section for the basics.

Hardware and Electronic Tools

For every well-stocked computer room, there are dozens of tools, toys, and "gotta-haves." In order to assess what your real needs are—as opposed to what your budget might be—let's look at a variety of technologies that can be extremely useful to the computer crafter. Read through the descriptions, check out magazines and catalogs, and put together your wish list. Prioritize based on your individual needs. Here are the items we find to be most useful.

A **digital camera** does not use film! Instead, the image is saved on a memory card and this information can be transferred directly into your computer.

A **fax modem** allows you to receive and send faxes from within your computer. Any item that you have stored electronically can be sent to another fax machine, either a stand-alone fax or a computer-based fax. If you wish to send something that is not already stored on your computer, you must scan it first, then send it. Anyone who can send a fax can send it to your computer. To read the fax, you can view it on your screen or you can print it and review it.

The **hard drive** provides internal digital storage on your computer for permanent (as permanent as computers get)

space to save images, documents, programs, and your computer's operating system.

A **scanner** is a device for creating a digital image from an existing printed or photographed image. Scanners generally consist of a flat glass panel upon which you place your hard-copy image, then close the cover over the art. The internal light runs over the artwork, capturing the colors as digital representations. You can scan any object that can be safely placed on the glass panel: text pages, artwork, small three-dimensional objects, fabric, books, photographs, and so on. Scanners come bundled with software that allows for either a stand-alone application or an image-editing program like Adobe Photoshop to process the image.

Software

Because each software program is different and each release of a particular type of program will vary, we cannot give explicit step-by-step descriptions of how to accomplish the action on your individual program. We have provided general information on where the functions are usually found, in what types of programs and within particular programs. We have also included alternative methods and synonymous terms, to help you figure out your programs' capabilities.

Background textures are electronically rendered images that cover a large area and can be used to fill in an overall design. The software that creates these textures takes some very simple beginning material: maybe a few blobs of color or a snippet of a scanned image. Using powerful algebraic equations, the software converts these pieces of input into very complex patterns. You can easily turn one of these computer-generated designs into a desktop pattern for your computer. Save the pattern as a file. If you are using a Mac, open your Control Panel and click on "Desktop Patterns." Select the image and copy it, then paste it into the "Desktop Patterns" window. That's it! For Windows users, place your image in the "Windows/Systems" folder with ".bmp" as an extension. Go back to your Control panel, select Display, locate your image in the dialog box. Click on it and away you go.

Clip art is available either through the Internet, CD-ROMs diskettes, or as part of a software package, such as drawing, painting, image-editing, page-layout, or other programs. Created by a publishing house or a graphic artist, the copyright-free images are generally either basic line drawings or color drawings, or they may be photographic scenes or isolated photographed objects with the background removed. (See the resources section, page 141, for Internet and mail order sources for free and inexpensive clip art.) Clip art may also be referred to as "stock" images or "content."

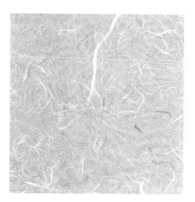

This interesting background texture is simply a scanned image of rice paper.

Clip art images can range from simple line drawings to more complex photographic scenes.

Drawing programs, also referred to as illustration software, allow you to draw basic shapes using vector mathematical processing to create scalable objects. Some common programs are Adobe Illustrator, CorelDRAW, FreeHand, and AppleWorks Draw.

Filters are add-on mini-programs that are part of such software as Adobe Photoshop and other imaging-editing programs. Filters perform the special role of adding interesting effects to an image. Common filters include functions that will apply ripples to an image so that it appears to be visible through gently waving water, or effects that radically change the colors within an image to make it look like a psychedelic poster from the 1960s.

Image-editing software is another name for a painting program.

Page-layout programs allow you to combine text and images to produce newsletters, brochures, and other page-oriented designs. These programs have strong text-manipulation capabilities: resizing, styling, shaping, and special effects such as wrapping text around pictures and oddly shaped graphics. PageMaker and Quark are the most common high-end brand names. You may also see Print Master and Print Shop bundled with entry-level PCs.

Painting programs, also called image-editing programs, create images via direct application of pixel after pixel on the screen, as in such software as Adobe Photoshop. These images depend on the "ppi" or "pixels per inch" to give them clarity. The more pixels per inch, the sharper the image, up to a certain practical limit. Almost all monitors display images at around 70–75 pixels per inch, so any image intended to be viewed on a screen (and not printed) need only be prepared at this resolution. See the section on image clarity (pages 12–13) for more information on how the ppi of an image affects printing.

Photo CD When you take a roll of film to be processed at your local store, you can ask for a CD-ROM to be made of the photographs as an alternative to glossy prints. The processor develops the film, encodes the images, and "burns" them onto a CD-ROM. When you load it in your CD drive you can use either the enclosed "viewer" or your image-editing software to view the picture on screen. You can then edit it and save it to your hard drive.

Photo image-editing program is another term for a painting program.

Viewer software, usually given away free with photo CDs, clip art collections, and some bundled hardware

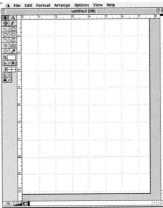

Drawing programs (illustration software) enable you to create line art; painting programs (image-editing software) let you manipulate photographs and other images.

Claris Draw

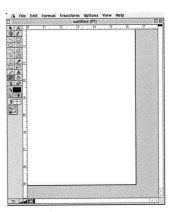

Claris Paint

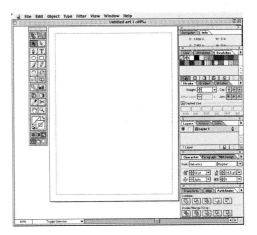

Adobe Ilustrator

Adobe Photoshop

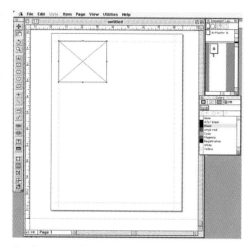

Quark Xpress

Applying a "wave" filter to the scanned rice paper yielded this effect.

offerings, comprises small programs that allow limited viewing capability of images. They do not have the breadth and depth of a program like Adobe Photoshop, the premier image-editing software.

Basic Tools and Commands

The following terms refer to various functions that can be applied to objects and other aspects of your images.

Acquire brings up the scanner software to process the photograph or object sitting on the scanner glass. In Adobe Photoshop, for instance, using "File," "Import," "Acquire" brings up the scanner software window.

Align, which is available in many draw or layout programs, lines up the tops, bottoms, or sides of objects; centers objects relative to one another; or spaces a series of objects over a given area. Because of the mathematical capabilities of a drawing program, very accurate alignment is possible.

Attributes refers to the style or look of an object. For text, it might include the size, color, or whether the text is bold or italic. For a box, it might include what the box is filled with, what color the line around the box is, and how wide that line is.

Borders and patterns can each be created both in painting programs and in drawing programs. The filters that come with your painting program allow you to take a very simple splash of a few colors and manipulate them to create whirls, crystallized color areas, clouds, or other designs. In drawing programs the approach is more mechanical: draw an object, then copy and paste it repeatedly to form a pleasing design.

Brush, pen, and pencil tools encompass all sorts of mark-makers in drawing programs. Some programs have spray paint tools, chalk tools, specialized texturing tools, and even tools that act like a particular artist's brushwork. The general principle is that you select the thickness of the stroke, the color, the opacity (see below), and other attributes. The tool keeps these attributes until the next time you change them, so moving from one tool to another will bring you to the characteristics that were last selected.

Center refers to the placement of a picture, line, shape, or any other object in the middle of another space or shape.

Clean up, also called "retouching images," is the first step when you acquire an image from a scanner. When you look at the scan on your monitor you may find that the color is off (too red, too blue, or the like), or that a stray hair or piece of dust landed on the scanner glass, or perhaps that there were imperfections in the original. For example, old photographs may have scratches or bent corners. You can fix all of these imperfections with a variety of tools in your image-editing or painting program. Almost every program of this type offers information on this in their tutorials, so check your user manual for more specific examples.

Copy/Paste refers to software's ability to duplicate an object and repeat it identically elsewhere. You select something (a piece of text, an image, or other object), copy it, and then paste it into another location or document. Most software is consistent in the keystrokes used to invoke these functions. On the Mac, "Copy" is achieved with the Command key (sometimes called the Apple or Butterfly key because of the key's symbol shown on the keyboard) plus the "C" key; and "Paste" is accomplished with Command key plus the "V" key. On Wintel machines, use the Control key plus the "C" key for "Copy" and the Control key plus the "V" key for "Paste."

Compositing *See* "Layer/condense/collage."

Crop refers to eliminating an outer area of an image that doesn't enhance your design. The crop tool is used to define the rectangular portion of an image that you wish to keep.

Drawing tools are what is used in drawing and painting programs, which all draw simple lines. The thinnest line is generally referred to as a hairline stroke. (See "Brush, pen, and pencil tools" for more specifics about line effects.) The ruled line elements in drawing programs can often be styled with arrows at one or both ends, colors, dashed lines, and other attributes. Perfect horizontal or vertical lines can be drawn by holding down the Shift key in almost any software. Another command that applies to lines is "set stroke to none," which changes any line you have drawn to transparent so you will see only the colored area of, for instance, a box or a circle, but not the outline around it.

Eraser tool has the ability to wipe out entire sections of an image in an image-editing or painting program, allowing you to carefully edit out parts of a photograph or to isolate chosen objects. You can usually change the size and shape of the eraser. Other tools that can be used to erase extraneous parts of the picture are the lasso tool and the selection tool. This process is also known as "knocking out the background" or "removing sections of an image."

Fill refers to the fact that any object created in a drawing program can be filled in with patterns or with color. Pattern fills can either be created and added to a library or selected from the options offered by the software. Typical fills are stripes, brick wall designs, and dots.

Flip/Flop Most software has the ability to flip an image on an axis, defined as the midpoint of the selected object. You can turn it upside down or from left to right. This is especially helpful in preparing graphics to print using T-shirt transfers because the transfer process naturally reverses everything. Also called "reversing images."

Group refers to the ability of most drawing software to group several items together, allowing you to lock in their position relative to one another. You can then drag the whole gang of items to a new location all together. An additional benefit in some instances is the ability to

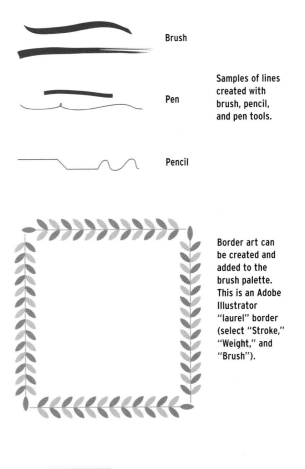

Samples of lines created with brush, pencil, and pen tools.

Border art can be created and added to the brush palette. This is an Adobe Illustrator "laurel" border (select "Stroke," "Weight," and "Brush").

This pattern was created with a series of triangles in Adobe Illustrator, and was then added to the pattern library (select drawing, "Edit," and "Define Pattern"). It is then available for use in your swatch palette.

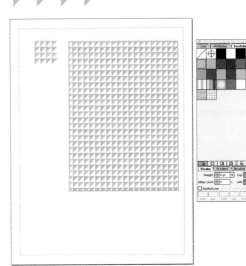

In most image-editing software, eliminating the background is as easy as selecting the eraser tool and erasing!

The image on the left is the original orientation; the one in the center is the flopped version; the one on the right is the original flipped upside down.

| Original | Flopped (horizontal) | Flipped (vertical) |

Image-editing software allows you to create layers, so you have more freedom to combine images, blend them, and experiment with transparency.

change all of the attributes of the entire group at the same time. For example, if you draw several boxes and group them, you can then change their colors, the width of the outline stroke, and other characteristics all at once.

Join/Unite/Combine Some drawing programs allow you to combine two objects into one. For example, a circle and a triangle could be joined to make a new shape. Check your software; sometimes you can combine shapes while leaving out overlapping parts, intersecting parts, and other more complicated choices.

Lasso is a selection tool. In your painting program, draw the lasso around the area you want to edit in order to select it. The lasso can be rather finely manipulated. (Compare this with "Magic wand.")

Layer/condense/collage are tools in image-editing and painting programs that let you separate out parts of one picture and combine them with others. If your editing program is capable of separating an image into layers, you can easily create collages and other effects with more control. When you use this layering capability, the software acts as if each image sits on an invisible sheet of plastic stacked one on top of another, which you can then rearrange, add to, delete, and edit individually. When you have completed your composition, you must "collapse" the layers and merge them all into one layer. If you don't, your image will retain tons of information and the size of your file will be unnecessarily inflated, which will greatly slow down any other computer processing you wish to complete, such as printing or storing. The layering function is sometimes called "compositing."

Magic wand is a tricky tool that can be very helpful for selecting large, similarly colored areas in painting programs. You can ask a magic wand tool to pick out large areas of color by setting the tolerances fairly high. If you are searching for a distinct shade, you can crank down the settings very tightly. The tool searches contiguous areas for any shade that matches that intensity. Some more sophisticated programs let you select noncontiguous areas and also have other settings to increase the tool's flexibility.

Object refers to each element you create in a drawing program. An object can be edited individually or grouped with other objects.

Opacity refers to the ability to alter the transparency of all or part of an image in a painting program, from 100 percent (no transparency at all) to anything above 0 percent. You can layer images and blur edges so they seem to blend together, or make your composition look as if you can see right through one image to the image layer beneath. *See also* "Brush, pen, and pencil tools" and "Layer/condense/collage."

Open/Open Image are two different concepts. Virtually every software program allows you to create a new file or document by using your "File" and "New" commands. When you open a new document, most software reveals a blank page that has the same characteristics as the last document you worked on. By contrast, when you open an image, you are asking the software to resort to an image that's already on your hard drive or on the CD-ROM in your CD drive.

Paste *See* "Copy/Paste."

Patterns *See* "Borders and patterns."

Print This action allows the printer to review your computer's internal information and print a copy of the image on paper. It sounds simple, but there is a degree of complexity here. First, your printer must be installed properly, with the associated drivers and proper fonts installed. Then, when you request a print action, there are a number of choices to make, depending on the brand and model of your equipment. You will probably be able to chose the number of prints, whether they are collated, what paper orientation is to be used (landscape or portrait; see "Paper orientation," page 33), and whether you are printing in color or black and white. See page 22 for information about printing on both sides of the paper.

Resize is a function of all drawing and painting programs that allows you to alter the size of your images. You select an object, then drag the corner point of the object to stretch or shrink it to the desired dimensions.

Retouching is another term for "clean up."

Revert or undo commands can be used interchangeably or may mean slightly different things, depending on the program. Generally they are both used when you want to back up to an earlier version of your work.

Rotate lets you twirl that photo 180 degrees, 90 degrees, or any number you wish. Some software limits you to whole numbers; others lets you spin things freehand; still others offer several methods of rotating.

Save and Save As commands are slightly different from each other. "Save" simply stores the changes that you have made since the last save, while "Save As" creates a whole new copy of your image or document to the specified spot. Remember to save often! You can always use the undo commands or revert to older versions, but saving frequently is the best habit you can develop.

Set stroke to none *See* "Drawing tools."

Select/Drag/Position are related commands. Dragging your mouse vertically over an area will either select that rectangular area (in a painting program) or select all the images within that area (in a drawing program). To drag, select an object, hold your mouse button down, and move the mouse to a new location. Let go of the mouse button and the image is now in a new position.

Shape tools offer a variety of options in drawing programs. With the **box** tool you can create either rectangles or squares. In almost every software program, holding down the shift key while you drag your cursor to make the box will give you a perfect square. The **ellipse** tool lets you draw ovals, or hold down the shift key while drawing to create perfect circles instead of elliptical objects. For stars, octagons, polygons, and other fun shapes, use the **hexagonal** tool. If you'd like to make freeform shapes, use the **freehand** tool. Also called "drawing using points," the process consists of constructing shapes around specific points that can later be adjusted. Think of these shapes like a length of garden hose formed into a loop. You could move the hose around to create kidney shapes, loops, wiggles, or other forms, continuing to reshape the hose as your needs change. In the software, you will see the spots at which you can "grab" the shape and drag it to a new spot to adjust it.

Transparency *See* "Opacity."

Saving Images

Saving images refers to the crucial process of taking your work out of the volatile, RAM memory and placing it on disk storage, which is more permanent. Save your work often, since any glitch (such as a system crash or a power surge) will dump all the work that is in RAM. This will leave you with a file that reflects only the work you have done up to the point of the previous "Save." The type of image you are creating determines the way you will save it. Each file name is associated with a different type of software, generally the program that was used to create it. Knowing what you intend to do with the image and where it will be displayed will help you to determine the best file type for each image.

Bitmap versus vector Bitmaps are pixel-based photographs or painted images. Each image is composed of many small areas of color. If you enlarge an area of a photograph, you will eventually see that the picture is really made up of many small squares (or pixels) of color, one color to a square. In vector images, made in drawing or page-layout programs, each object is like a fluid, continuous shape. It looks the same whether it is 1 inch or 10 inches across. This is because the software is mathematically drawing each image to scale, and it then fills in the outline with whatever you have asked for. Vector images look more hard-edged and you can always count on them to change scale gracefully.

Image formats are varied. In a laundry list of popular and not-so-popular formats, the most common ones are **EPS**, a vector-based image; **TIFF**, a bitmap (pixel-based) format, used widely in paint programs; **JPEG**, a bitmapped image in a compressed format, useful for sending across the Internet; and **PICT**, which is frequently used for clip art.

Import is one of the biggest areas for potential problems and frustration in all of softwaredom. Depending on what software you are heading to and from, sometimes you can bring one type of image into a program that doesn't generally use that format, but you should never wait till you are under a deadline to test your assumptions. Generally, though, products from a single manufacturer

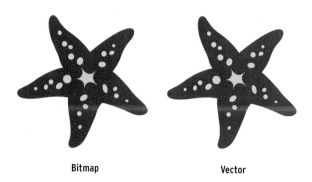

| Bitmap | Vector |

Bitmapped images are composed of pixels, which become evident when the picture is enlarged. At this size, the pixels can only be seen under magnification, and are most apparent around the edges. Vector images are more fluid and maintain the same appearance even when greatly enlarged.

(such as Adobe) work well together, especially if everything was created on the same platform (either Mac or Wintel).

Resolution is measured both on the screen and in printing. Most monitors have resolutions around 70–75 dpi. Scanning resolutions at about 100 to 150 dpi are more than adequate for most projects. Even though your printer capability may be as high as 1440 dpi, your eye will not detect much difference in scans that are created at higher resolutions.

Scanning at ever-larger resolutions dramatically increases the image size and makes some images unworkable in lower-end software programs. Many scanners and some clip art will create files at very high resolutions, up to 2400 dpi, but for most of us this is overkill. Try this test: find a photograph with a resolution of 300 dpi and print it. Change the resolution to 200 dpi. Does it look substantially different on the screen? Print it and compare it to the earlier print. Can you tell the difference? Change the resolution to 100 dpi and perform the same comparisons. Continue to test to find the right resolution for your screen and your printer. Lower resolutions mean smaller files; cutting the dpi in half makes a file just 25 percent of its original size.

Variations of an image are extremely useful to save. As you work on an image, you may want to save several different views. Sometimes the more you work on something, the less you like the results and it is great to have intermediate steps to jump back to. Often, too, these earlier versions can be useful in other projects. We tend to save everything, just in case. Develop a numbering and naming scheme that works for you. One that we have used includes the name of the main object in the picture and the date in this format: mmddyy. Several files from the same date get an A, B, C, and so on after the date. This way, your computer will sort them by date and by version.

Color Terminology

Color, of course, is one of the most important aspects of endeavors that ultimately result in printed images. Many variables have an impact on color, and what you see on the screen is not exactly what your printer will lay down. Following are explanations of some important color terms.

Color fidelity refers to the difference between what a color looks like on your monitor compared to how your printer renders it. Because monitors use the RGB scale (Red, Green, Blue) and printers use a scale called CMYK (Cyan, Magenta, Yellow and Black), there will never be a perfect match. Design houses spend a fortune on coming as close as possible for demanding clients who are paying huge dollars for a photograph to have the exact shade of red or just the right golden glow. For our purposes, any external devices or fancy software are unnecessary. Instead, make a test document and print it. This will show you what your printer thinks blue looks like, for instance, compared to what your monitor shows. Keep this as a reference. Note that this will also change over time and with the particular formulation of the printer inks. If color matching is very important, test the project before the final print. (See "Creating a Sample Book," pages 22–23, for more information about testing colors.)

Duotones lend a creative look to any image and are often used in commercial design. A duotone is a color photograph that has been manipulated so that the rainbow of hues are changed into two tones. Try using two very contrasting colors or odd shades of gray for interesting effects.

Gradients is a term referring to the differing intensity of a single color or a color range. A gradient is an area of color that starts at one edge or point in the object. The software calculates infinitesimal changes in the original color, with the deepest intensity at the starting point and then the color proceeds to fade out across the object. Some software allows you to combine several gradients into one object and to change the direction of the run of color. Programs like Kai's Power Tools (KPT) take this simple concept to amazing heights, creating gradients that look exactly like metal and other wild effects with the push of a few buttons.

Grayscale is the intermediate step between color and true black-and-white images. In this process of converting colors to one of 256 shades of gray, each individual color is not assigned a shade of gray, but each intensity of all colors is assigned a shade. This means that the darkest shades of all the colors in a photo become the darkest grays, and the lightest shades become the lightest grays. Pink and light blue become light gray, for example, while maroon and navy become dark gray.

Preselected palettes are generally included in most drawing programs, meaning there is a built-in palette of colors from which you can select. Often there are alternatives, such as the colors from the Pantone system or all the colors from the crayon box. Some programs allow you to set up a range of tones as the defaults when you open a new document. Others allow you to drag a color from anywhere on the desktop and put it on your palette, where it will be stored for future use.

Sepia toning allows you to convert any photograph into a turn-of-the-century image by using monotones and selecting a warm gray or blackish-brown color for the filtering. If you have a mix of old black-and-white as well as color images, you may want to change the color in all of them to a sepia tone and use them as a harmonious grouping.

Working with Text

A variety of tools and operations pertain to text. When using text as part of a creative project, it can become a highly decorative element—not simply a written expression but a visual one. Here are some of the key concepts.

Coloring text is a fun option to try out. We're used to seeing black text, but text can be any shade of the rainbow. For larger type sizes there can be two color elements: the outline can be one shade and the fill a different one.

Decorative capital letters add an elegant touch. You can buy software that re-creates the beautiful capitals that the monks painted in illuminated manuscripts. Clip art books are full of decorative capital letters, and the capitals are often included with software for making greeting cards.

Decorative fonts come in seemingly thousands of different typestyles, some quite wild. We've seen letters made of logs, Old English styles, graffiti, cartoon, ultramodern and many other varieties. Some fonts are free; some can be purchased from online and mail order sources. (See the resources section, page 141, for vendors.)

Dingbats and doodads are crazy little design elements that may be a typeface all of their own or may be invoked by special combinations of characters.

Point size can vary from practically illegible to humongous. Some programs limit the range of point sizes. Most text is 10 to 14 points for body copy and 12 to 20 for headline text. Be aware that a 10-point typeface in one style may be substantially smaller or larger than a 10-point typeface of a different design.

Serif versus sans serif describes the presence or absence of little curved strokes adorning each letter. These flourishes, called serifs, originated at the time when people still wrote with quill pens. Typestyles without these flourishes are sans serif (meaning without serif). Sans serif styles generally look more casual and modern to our eye; Helvetica is the most familiar. Times is a typical serif style and appears more formal.

Styling text can generally be accomplished by looking under the "Font," "Style," or "Format" menus and applying

To see gradients in action, try filling a box or any other object you've drawn with a continuous range of one color from white to the deepest shade of that color.

Here the same image is rendered in each of the five image types: four-color, black-and-white, duotone, sepia, and bitmap.

Large display fonts have areas that can be outlined with one color and filled with another.

✔ 🚲 🎁 🚋 ⊖ ⓘ ✦   **Webdings**

𝄢 𝄐 𝄞 ↗ ◺ ✢ ●   **Wingdings**

❀ ☆ ✩ ◆ ✛ ✜ ➞ ⑦ ●   **Zapf Dingbats**

Dingbats may be simple symbols or more elaborate themed motifs.

Color

Color

Color

Color

24 point type

36 point type

The text we are accustomed to reading is usually about 10 or 12 points in size, but display or decorative text is considerably larger. The first and third examples here are sans serif type; the second and fourth are serif style.

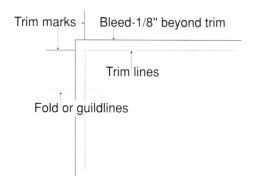

Interesting text effects can be achieved by using the feature that allows you to place type on an irregular path.

Trim marks · Bleed-1/8" beyond trim

Trim lines

Fold or guildlines

When indicating trim and fold lines on your printed piece, take care that they do not print on the "live" area of the object.

a variety of attributes. Try manipulating the look of a font with some of the unusual effects, such as shadow, outline, and strike through.

Templates are very useful if you want a document containing certain information to be readily accessible. Most word-processing software allows you to save a file as a template, which is a actually master document in which reside a set of chosen elements that you want to appear each time you open a new document. When you make a change, you'll save the new document with a new name and the next time you open the template it will appear exactly as before, in its original form. This is helpful when you would like to add the same information to many different documents, as for a fax cover sheet, for example. Even though some of the information (recipient's name and fax number, for instance) will change for each cover sheet you send, certain standard information (your name and fax number) will remain the same each time. By creating a template, this standard information is always available for a new document and does not have to be input each time.

Type on a path is a fun feature available in page-layout, drawing, and some image-editing programs that allows you to create a path (a box, an ellipse, a line) and then key in words. When the feature is applied, the text snakes around the edge of the line you have drawn.

Text tool allows you to type information on the image surface. In drawing programs, the text retains full editability. In painting programs, once the text has been incorporated into the image, it is often very hard to change, although newer programs make this easier.

Creating Layouts

This section explains terminology that relates to how you lay objects out on your page, both on the screen and on the printed paper. The terms stem from the world of magazine and advertising art, so they are rooted in a very old and exacting profession. The terms may be unfamiliar and sound a bit technical, so read through each one and refer to the illustrations to absorb the concepts.

Bleed is evident when you consider the cover of a magazine: the image generally flows right over the very edges of the page, extending the color or image beyond the trim lines. When you have given yourself this "bleed" or "fudge space," small variations in the trimming will leave you with paper color showing through where you wanted image!

Fold and cut lines The layouts shown in our projects often have lines to indicate where you will fold or cut out the printed image. Trim lines are shown solid, and fold or perforation lines appear as dashes or dotted lines.

Ganging up, or "two up," is a helpful feature when the item you wish to print is smaller than half the page. When more than one image needs to be printed, ganging up two

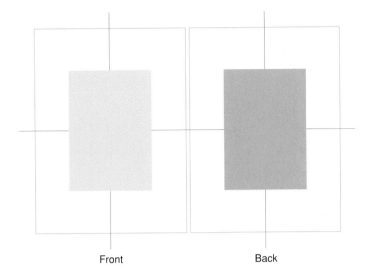
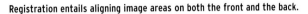

Front   Back

Registration entails aligning image areas on both the front and the back.

images on the same page into one layout is economical, saving both paper and time.

Guidelines are the first step when beginning a project. While you contemplate the blank page, guidelines (also known as a layout grid) will help you position your images or text.

Paper handling refers to the way your printer holds each sheet of paper as it travels along the paper path. The ink cannot be sprayed in these edge areas and in a small margin at the top and bottom of each sheet. Every model of every manufacturer has slightly different margins, sometimes called the **nonprint area.** There are two ways to check the maximum size of the printable area for your brand of printer. You can consult the manual for information about print specifications, which will tell you how much room the paper feeding-mechanism needs. Or, in a word-processing program, open a new document, set the margins at all four sides to "o," and type Xs along several lines at the top and bottom of the page, from the left edge to the right edge. Print this page, ignoring any system messages you may get stating that your image area is larger than your allowable printing space. When complete, you will see where the clipping occurred. Check these measurements and note them down for future reference. That will give you an accurate feel for where you can print on the page.

Paper orientation refers to the positioning of the paper for printing. Portrait, or vertical, orientation is an $8^1/_2$- x 11-sheet positioned in the usual fashion. Changing the orientation to landscape, or horizontal, means that the long edge is oriented to the horizon. The method by which you make

these choices may be slightly different for each software program, but the "File" menu usually offers commands that call up page-setup dialog boxes or print dialog boxes.

Registration refers to alignment of the elements in two documents so that when you print the first document on the front side, the second document will match up with it exactly when you print on the back side. *See also* "Trim marks" below.

Tiling is a technique that allows you to divide up an oversized file into pieces that are small enough to be printed on $8^1/_2$- x 11-inch sheets. The image is created on the computer as a whole, but since your printer is capable of printing only a fraction of the full finished size, the image is then broken into separate pages, or "tiles," and each one is printed on an individual sheet of paper. A huge drawing or photo can thus be split into many tiles, then after the final print each sheet is trimmed and the image reassembled. The tiling technique can also be used to make long banners or large pieces to cover a wall or a table. Not all software offers this capability, and those that do may each handle tiling very differently. Check the "Page Setup" areas and "Print" options for pointers.

Trim marks are lines indicating where a piece of paper will eventually be cut off. Generally, trim marks are placed outside your image area but when that is not possible, cut just inside the trim mark so that no lines remain on the finished object.

White ground is the background color when opening a new document. In some programs this may be changed to a transparent effect.

ESSENTIAL CRAFT SUPPLIES

At the beginning of each project you will find a list of the materials needed. Some of the items are common tools; others are specific to each project. Most products can be found in craft stores; anything unusual or hard to find is referenced in the resources section (pages 140–41).

Most of the projects can be accomplished with ordinary household tools and materials. Following is a roundup of the various tools and supplies we use in our projects, organized by type. If reasonable precautions are taken, many of these projects can be accomplished by children with adequate supervision; in particular, adults should perform the operations involving sharp or hot tools. And remember that certain supplies can have dangerous effects if used incorrectly, so always use spray products (adhesives, paints, fixatives, varnishes) only in a well-ventilated area.

Preparation Tools

- *Scrap paper* is great to have on hand. Keep mistakes and test prints to use in future projects, but save only the sheets that haven't been rippled by ink absorption.
- *Old newspaper*
- An *old phone book* makes an ideal small work surface for gluing and cutting. Just tear off the used surfaces and toss them out; each page is a new, clean surface.
- Small pieces of *scrap cloth*

Cutting Tools

- *Scissors:* No craft room would be complete without scissors, but remember that any cutting that requires precision, especially straight lines, should be cut with a blade.
- *Blades:* The materials lists in the projects generally call for a craft knife, but a utility or X-Acto knife or a rotary cutter will also generally work. Be sure to have plenty of new blades on hand and change them often so you're always working with a sharp one.
- *Self-healing cutting mat,* for use with any blades
- *Straightedge:* When cutting straight lines, always use a blade tool against a straightedge.
- *Paper cutter:* Although not essential, a paper cutter is useful for many projects.

Marking Tools

- *Paints:* acrylic, gouache, watercolor
- *Paintbrushes:* Keep a variety of types and sizes on hand. Sometimes disposable brushes are the best choice, especially for glues, varnishes, and polyurethane.
- *Dimensional paint* comes in lots of colors and a variety of thicknesses. It's fun to use and adds a bit of texture to many projects.
- *Colored pencils*
- *Markers*
- *Pencil*
- *Scoring tools:* To achieve a nice, crisp fold line, it is essential to score the line before folding. The materials lists generally call for a bone folder (a slim tool resembling a letter opener), but other scoring devices can be used with relatively equal success, such as an empty ball point pen, a rolling ball burnisher, the back (noncutting) edge of a craft knife blade, even a butter knife. Any scoring device should be used against a straightedge when scoring a straight line.

Embellishments

- *Crimping device:* This cute hand-held clamp will evenly pleat a piece of paper.
- *Embossing fluid* works with a *heat gun* to add dimension to an image.
- *Rubber stamps and inks*
- *Decorative edgers or pinking shears*
- *Decorative corner edger*
- *Sealing wax and seal*
- *Die cuts:* These colorful and neatly cut paper shapes (originally designed for scrapbooking and stamping), including stars, teddy bears, hearts, letters, and numbers, can be used in myriad ways. Add them to collages; laminate, paint, and decorate them; even print on the larger ones.

Adhering Tools

- *Tape:* cellophane, double-sided, masking, library binding
- *Glue:* white, household, Aleene's Tacky Glue™, rubber cement
- *Glue sticks* are often easier to work with than traditional glues.
- *DryLine* is an adhesive in a tape-dispenser device, very popular with paper artists.
- *Hot glue gun and glue sticks:* Low-temperature or dual-temperature models are best for paper projects; the high-temp models get very hot indeed.
- *Decoupage glue:* Probably best known by the Mod Podge brand, this can be brushed on as both an adhesive and a finishing coat.
- *Spray adhesive*
- *Double-stick foam pads*

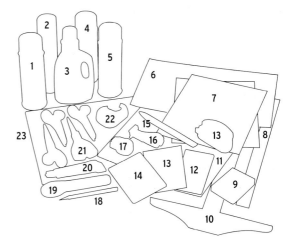

1. Polyurethane	7. Self-adhesive laminating film	13. Removable mounting squares	19. Rotary cutter
2. Static guard	8. Metal ruler/straightedge	14. Two-sided mounting tape	20. Utility knife
3. Fabric softener	9. Brass fasteners	15. Bone folder	21. Decorative edging scissors
4. Artist's fixative	10. T-square	16. Rubber band clamps	22. Two-sided tape
5. Spray adhesive	11. Firm ironing surface (tile)	17. Decorative corner punch	23. Self-healing cutting mat
6. Printable fabric sheets	12. Reusable mounting adhesive	18. X-Acto knife (craft knife)	

Measuring Tools

- *Ruler:* Choose an all-metal ruler or a wooden ruler with a metal edge so that in addition to measuring, it can be used as a straightedge when cutting or scoring.

Assembling Tools

- *Ribbon*
- *C-clamps*
- *Wide rubber bands*
- *Iron*
- *Ironing board,* or other firm, heat-resistant surface
- *Pins* or basting thread and needle
- *Sewing machine*
- *Thread*
- *String*
- Thin sheet of *acrylic*
- *Dowels* or thin wooden strips

Finishing Tools

- *Boards:* Bristol board, cardboard, foam core, and poster board are used as a support surface for mounting printed images that require some structure.
- *Artist's fixative*
- *Polyurethane or varnish,* either spray-on or paint-on type
- *Self-laminating film* or clear contact paper to protect printed images

Fabric Sheet Supplies

The Graphics Jacket project (pages 107–11) requires certain supplies to make fabric sheets that feed directly into the printer:
- *Downy Fabric Softener™*
- *Large sealable plastic bag*
- *Anti-static spray*
- *Plastic-coated freezer paper*

And now, on to the projects!

☐ Standard Booth (4
☐ Double Booth (4' x 10')
☐ PREMIUM SITE (first two rows inside
- additional $20

Name_____
Address_____
Telephone_____

All-County ANNUAL SWAP
Come and turn the conten
your attic into cash!

Saturday and Sunday, October 2
Fairgrounds   1234 Elm Street
From 7 AM to Dusk

Send in the attached Booth
reservation form to hold your spac
FULL PAYMENT DUE OCTOBER 15

County Swap Meet
12 Main Street
Hometown, USA 12345

Happy-Birthday
from
Great-Aunt Laurel

Isabel

STREET
O, CA 93333

Come help
MATTHEW
Celebrate his Eighth Birthday
on an African Safari
12 Noon
August 23 rd
1256 Oak Street,
Saturday
RSVP (919) 234-5678

day
Safari
23 rd
6 Oak Street
(919) 234-5678   12 Noon

CHAPTER TWO

paper projects

BOOKMARK

What You'll Need

MATERIALS
High-quality paper
Self-laminating plastic

TOOLS
Craft knife
Ruler or straightedge
Self-healing cutting mat
Bone folder
Rubber cement or white glue

ART
Scanned images, clip art,
 decorative fonts, dingbats

SOFTWARE
Page-layout and image-editing
 programs

SKILL LEVEL
Easy

COMPLETION TIME
1 hour

This is the perfect project to showcase a collection of unusual, fancy, or exotic typefaces as well as clip art and photographs you have been collecting. Scan family photographs that are particularly meaningful to someone special. Try a photo of your pet with the "vital statistics" printed below, or create an illustration or type treatment of your own in a drawing or painting program. Have fun with this project by personalizing gifts for everyone on your holiday list.

1. For the front of your bookmark, scan or create images or gather clip art. (We used three rose photographs, captured on a digital camera in a friend's garden.) Save your images in a format that you can import into a drawing or page-layout program. The finished bookmark is 2 x 6 inches, so size your images to fit comfortably in that space.

2. Lay out your bookmarks centered on an 11- x 8½-inch page, landscape orientation, which will make two bookmarks. **(See Illustration A.)** Indicate a center line (shown in red) and lay out the trim lines for four 2- x 6-inch boxes. Draw a rectangle, allowing for a ⅛ inch bleed all around (2¼ x 6¼ inch). Fill it with a solid color (we chose pink). Copy and paste three more rectangles into place. Make sure all four bottom edges are aligned. Some software has a special feature that allows for automatic alignment of objects; look in your software manual for "Align objects" instructions.

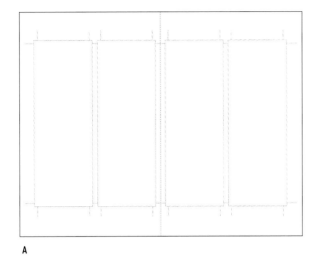

A

B

3. Within the first rectangle, create a box with "torn" edges either by using a filter effect in your editing program or by adding multiple points to a drawn box and moving the points individually to create a ragged edge. Copy and paste two more boxes below the first, positioning them so that all three are equally spaced within the pink rectangle. Also paste three "torn" boxes in each of the other two rectangles, to which text will be added later.

4. Import the three images into your layout. **(See Illustration B.)** Check your image-editing software to find out how to apply the torn-edge effect. Here we took the selection created by our torn image and deleted the rose image that extended beyond the selection, using the software commands "Invert selection" and "Delete." Copy and paste the images into the second rectangle, checking your alignment.

5. Using your text tool, add a caption or a relevant quote, styling it to look pleasing within the "torn" boxes. Use dingbats or other decorative elements to embellish the letters. We used the typeface "Cochin" with an element from "Botanical." **(See Illustration C.)**

(continued on next page)

C

Creativity

- Look for images in photo albums, your children's drawings, and themed clip art. Adapt borders or use interesting background textures that will highlight a special message.

- Add decorative flourishes from a symbol font, a Zapf Chancery font, or any of the many available clip art collections or fonts (see the resources guide).

- Continue to experiment with the size and even the shape of your bookmark. Just be sure it measures no more than about eight inches in length or it will be too long for most paperbacks and even some hardbound books.

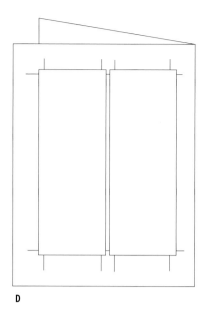

D

6. Print the bookmarks on high-quality paper. Remember to orient the paper properly. Let the printout dry for a few minutes.

7. Score the fold exactly down the center, fold on the score line, and crease with the bone folder. **(See Illustration D.)** Glue the two sides together. With the craft knife and straightedge, trim the bookmark to its finished size. (A paper cutter or rotary cutter also works well for this.)

8. Cut two pieces of self-laminating plastic at least $1/2$ inch bigger in both length and width than your bookmark. Peel off the backing paper from one piece of the plastic. Carefully place the image face up on the adhesive side. Peel the backing off the second piece of plastic and carefully position it over the bookmark. **(See Illustration E.)** Rub the pieces firmly to make sure the laminate adheres, eliminating air bubbles as you smooth it out. Repeat the laminating process for the second bookmark.

9. Trim all sides of the laminate to $1/8$ or $1/4$ inch bigger than the bookmarks. **(See Illustration F.)** Clean the edges and round off the corners to protect them from splitting.

E

F

INVITATIONS AND POSTCARDS

The concept of mail art entails sending creative letters and cards that are small works of art. Some unlikely objects have become mail art: coconuts, metal postcards, even Lucite boxes filled with collaged materials. We love to send ourselves postcards. We make up funny designs and pop them into the mail. Try mailing yourself a postcard on a good day so you'll remember your upbeat mood a few days later. Pass the cards along to other folks or keep them in a shoebox for a rainy day.

Business uses of cards are endless. It pays to draw clients' attention to your name, so invent reasons to send out cards, like National Postcard Day. Repeat mailings are the best way to build brand-name awareness. Send one a month, for ongoing coverage.

The four projects here—invitations, business postcards, postcards with a return mailer, and reminders—offer plenty of opportunities to create your own unique mail art. Just be sure the card stock you chose will fit in your printer!

Invitations

It is always fun to make plans for a party. Your own personalized party invitations are so much nicer than the corny ones found in stores. You can establish the party theme with this initial notice, then follow through with party decor (see "Pin the Tail on the Zebra," pages 84–87).

1. Open a new document and create a page layout to the dimensions of your card, keeping in mind your printer margins. Select clip art or create your own drawings to reflect your party theme. In your drawing or page-layout program, assemble the art and copy for the front of the card. Position your art within the postcard dimension boundaries.

2. On the reverse, indicate the positioning of the stamp, type your return address, and leave a space for the recipient's name and address. Experiment with colors, type styles, and perhaps a small graphic to coordinate with your overall theme.

3. Print as many copies as you need plus a few extras. Allow to dry for a few minutes. If you are not using precut card blanks, trim your cards to size with a craft knife and straightedge.

4. Once you've addressed the invitations, get some really cool stamps—after you've put this much thought into it, have fun with this last detail!

What You'll Need

MATERIALS
Card stock or blank postcards

TOOLS
Craft knife
Straightedge
Self-healing cutting mat
Bone folder
Interesting postage stamps

ART
Computer graphics, clip art, decorative fonts

SOFTWARE
Page-layout program

SKILL LEVEL
Intermediate

COMPLETION TIME
Invitations: 1½ hours
Business postcards: 2 hours
Postcards with return: 3 hours
Reminders: ½ hours

Tip

Remember that a postcard can be read by people for whom it is not intended. Depending on where you live, think twice about sending kids' invitations without envelopes. This invitation can work just as well inside an envelope—which makes another surface to decorate!

Tips

• If you set up your card as shown in **Illustration A,** you can make two complete cards by feeding the stock back through the printer to print a front and a back each time. This is called "work-in-turn" and requires only one document for a complete card.

• If you have a computerized mailing list, you can reload the cards and print the mailing addresses. (Make sure the cards are properly aligned in the printer.) Or print the addresses on clear self-adhesive labels and stick them on the individual cards.

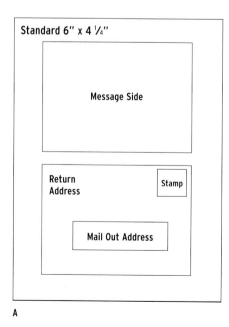

A

Business Postcards

These are designed to be sent on a regular basis to prospective or established customers to remind them that you are waiting to serve them. This inexpensive and catchy idea is actually a series of postcards. You send one a week to pique people's curiosity, then the final card reveals the big surprise (in this case, a blowout sale). Before you print them all, take a sample to your post office to ensure that the dimensions meet with postal regulations. For a really quick and easy project, just buy prestamped blank postcards!

1. Open a new document and create a page layout to the dimensions of your card, keeping in mind your printer margins. Set up the front and back as shown in **Illustration A.** The largest card that qualifies for postcard postage is 6 x 4¹/₄ inches, which will fit two on one page. If you are using precut postcard stock, adjust these measurements to match the template that comes with the postcard stock.

2. Type the number 5 and size it to fill the space. We placed the name of the store on this side. Use color to make it interesting, but keep it simple.

3. For the reverse, lay out your return address and the addressee information. (If you are printing on both sides, remember to center the template on the page: top to bottom and left to right so they will register correctly when you print the second side.) Again you can

dress it up with color, but keep the tints light so they don't interfere with the postal scanning machines. That also means there should be no copy across the bottom ¹/₂ inch of the card on the address side, where the post office places bar codes. Save this document both as "#5" and again as your master.

4. For each of the other cards (4, 3, and 2), open up your master page and repeat the design process, adjusting the color to make them different.

5. For the final card, place your message inside a big bang explosion box. Position the mailing information as above.

6. Print all your cards, allow to dry, and trim them out if necessary. You now have an inexpensive marketing campaign that hits a key point in advertising: build interest over time.

Postcards with a Return

This mailer is printed on card stock, which is folded and taped closed for sending. Remember, recipients are going to tear off half the mailer and send it back, thus the key to success is to plan your layout carefully so that all necessary information also appears on the retained half. For example, if they are signing up for a seminar, remember that they will need the time, place, date, and other pertinent information on the remaining piece. Another nice touch is to print the recipient's name and address twice on each card—once in the mailing address spot, and once on the return mailer. That makes it even easier for the potential customer to return the appropriate half.

Plan your layout on scrap paper first, following our diagrams as a guide. Make a "dummy," a small mockup of the actual piece, and note what will appear on which panel. Then test the layout until everything works.

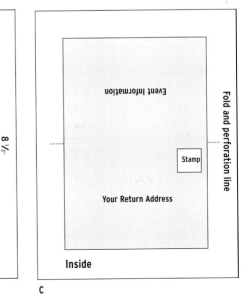

1. For the outside of the card, open a new document and create a page layout that is $8^1/_2$ x 11 inches. Remember to calculate your printer margins. Draw guidelines—lay out the outside dimensions for a 6- x 8 $^1/_2$-inch card. Bisect the layout at the halfway point to indicate the fold line. **(See Illustration B.)** If you are using precut, prescored paper stock, create your document to the size of the template included with the stock.

2. Create another page layout of the same dimensions for the card's inside. Position your interior text messages and art within these boundaries, with all the event information on the top half and your return address on the lower half. **(See Illustration C.)**

3. For the side with the mail-out layout, locate where the stamp, your return address, and the addressee information will be placed. If you are using a prepaid indicia, place that as shown in the diagram. Include some text or a small graphic to attract attention. Since this is a fold-over piece, you will need to rotate the text on the top half 180 degrees so it will read properly when folded. (Consult your software manual for specifics on rotating text and images.) In the lower panel, place the form that the addressee will fill out and to return to you. Print a draft, then trim and fold it to make sure all the information is aligned properly.

4. Print as many copies as you need plus a few extras. Allow to dry. With a craft knife and straight-edge, trim the cards to size, then score them for folding.

Outside

6"

Mail-Out Label or Address Imprint Area

Stamp

Your Return Address

8 ½"

Response Information

B

Inside

Event Information

Fold and perforation line

Stamp

Your Return Address

C

Creativity

Include a scanned photograph of yourself or add a small item like a colorful paper clip along with this. It is an inexpensive device for jogging people's memories—much more effective than a sticky note!

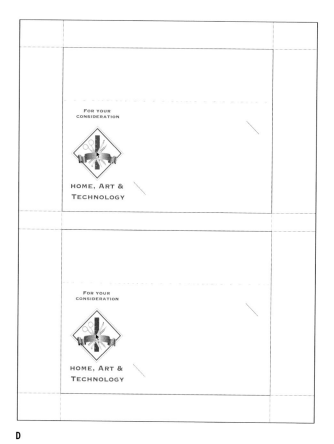

Reminders

Continue placing your business name in front of clients with these little attention-getters. If you see an article someone might like, make a photocopy and attach this card to it. Or send these out with the marketing materials in lieu of a more formal cover letter. Companies like Paper Direct (800-272-7377) sell the slit maker, or you can do it with a craft knife and a self-healing mat.

1. Open a new document and create a page layout for two 6- x 4$^1/_2$-inch cards. Draw a horizontal line 1$^1/_2$ inches from the top to indicate the fold line. **(See Illustration D.)**

2. In the remaining space, lay out your text and graphics. With a faint line, indicate where the business card slits will be.

3. Print up a number of reminders to keep on hand.

4. Cut the slits using a slit maker or a craft knife and straightedge. Score the fold line, but don't fold the cards until you need them.

5. When you want to use one, fold the card on the scored line and clip it to the materials to be sent with the business card facing out. People will know at a glance where it came from.

D

SHADOWBOX GREETING CARD

It's fun to make cards that have a bit of dimensionality. This one is a little different from most 3-D cards because it is more like a little shadowbox than a card. We achieved a romantic look with ridged cardboard and beautiful florals. You could try some of the bright cardboard colors available at art and craft stores. Consider using some of the unusual papers found in stationery stores, online and mail-order catalogs, and art supply shops.

You will be creating a three-dimensional image and framing it in a shallow box that has a cover. The color printer makes building three-dimensional effects easier because it readily allows you to reproduce multiple images in the colors, sizes, and quantities you need. Follow our dimensions or adjust the card to fit your image and your taste.

Allow yourself a little more time for this project and pay attention to accuracy. You'll be pleased with the results! And don't forget to look in the creativity section for more great ways to use these techniques.

What You'll Need

MATERIALS
Decorative card stock
Colorful corrugated cardboard
Rice paper
High-quality plain bond paper

TOOLS
Scissors
Craft knife
Straightedge
Self-healing cutting mat
Bone folder
Rubber cement or white glue
Double-sided foam pads

ART
Scanned photograph, clip art,
   decorative fonts

SOFTWARE
Page-layout and image-editing
   programs

SKILL LEVEL
Advanced

COMPLETION TIME
1½ hours, plus drying time

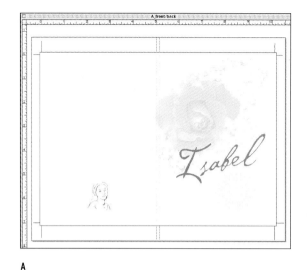

A

B

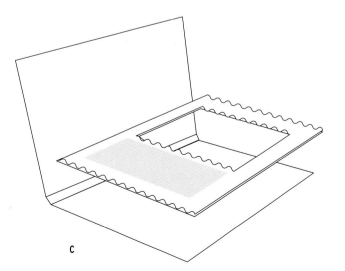

C

1. For a card measuring 5 x 7 inches when folded, create an 11- x 8^1/$_2$-inch document and lay out a rectangle 10^1/8 inches wide by 7 inches high, centered on the page. Place two guidelines down the center for the ^{1}/8-inch-capacity fold. Place the trim marks for the outer dimensions. **(See Illustration A.)** Save this as the master document. (You can keep referring back to this to make a variety of cards.)

2. Lay out the elements you want to print on the front of the card and save this document as "Card Outside." (For our design, we converted our flower to grayscale and then used a 20 percent tint for the outside of the card.)

3. Select an image for the three-dimensional insert. Look for one with some depth; a basket of flowers or a group of people works well.

4. Open a duplicate of the master document and save it as Card Inside. Create a 3- x 2^1/$_2$-inch window area centered in the upper half of the right side. Adjust the color and shape of your chosen image to suit your composition and size it to fit the window, positioning it so that the desired portion is within the 3 by 2^1/$_2$-inch window area. **(See Illustration B.)** (Note on the finished card how we allowed a few bits of the image to overlap the opening—it adds a nice touch.). Place some graphics and perhaps some decorative text on the left side.

D

5. Print the front of the card on card stock. Choose paper with interesting flecks to make the piece more unusual. Reload the paper and print the inside. (Be sure to reload correctly—check the printer manual or do a test run first.)

6. Score along the two center fold lines. Fold and crease with a bone folder.

7. Cut a piece of corrugated cardboard $1/4$ inch smaller all around than the dimensions of your folded card ($4^3/4$ x $6^3/4$ inches). Cut a 3- x $2^1/2$-inch opening, positioned $7/8$ inch from the left, top, and right edges of the cardboard. Glue the cardboard to the inside card back, with the window opening aligned over the image. **(See Illustration C.)**

8. Print a little message or greeting on rice paper. Tear the edges to give a deckle effect and glue it below the window. (Or glue in a blank piece of decorative paper and sign your name.)

9. Paste two copies of your chosen 3-D image onto a new document page and print this on high-quality paper. Allow to dry thoroughly.

10. Decide which parts of the image will be foreground and middle ground. For the middle, cut away most of the background from one of the images, leaving a little around the central portion. Trim the other image, leaving only the primary motif. **(See Illustration D.)**

11. Place two or three double-sided foam pads on the back of each trimmed image. If the pads are too large, cut them up. Peel off the protective paper and position the larger trimmed image. You will see the image begin to take on a dimensional effect, especially if a portion pops out of the frame. Use markers to color the edges if any of the white paper shows. Position the top image. **(See Illustration E.)**

E

POSTAGE STAMPS

What You'll Need

MATERIALS
Self-adhesive paper, preferably
   in letter-size sheets

TOOLS
Craft knife
Decorative-edge scissors

ART
Digitized photographs, decorative fonts

SOFTWARE
Page-layout and image-editing
   programs

SKILL LEVEL
Easy

COMPLETION TIME
1 hour

The Australian government is experimenting with putting ordinary citizen's photos on postage stamps—with this project we get the jump on them! Of course, these cannot be used as real stamps, but they are fun to attach to mail art projects, the backs of envelopes, and other missives.

You can make your stamps in any dimensions. Look for full-sized sheets of self-adhesive paper in large stationery stores. If you can only find smaller 4- x 6-inch pieces, plan your stamp images accordingly, making sure that you calculate the printer margins for your particular model.

Go wild with the graphics. Here we used pictures of our nieces, nephews, and pets, scanned from photographs. You can also use pictures from a photo CD or other sources. Of course, you can also make your own designs. Remember, the object is to keep it small and stamplike, so plan accordingly. Challenge your creativity with how much information you can deliver in such a small space.

A

B

1. To determine the size of your stamp, plan a grid on scratch paper before you get started. On an $8^{1}/_{2}$- x II-inch page, discounting the space for the printer margins, we were able to align 6 columns and 7 rows of stamps per page, for a finished postage stamp size of $I^{1}/_{4}$ x $I^{1}/_{2}$ inches. **(See Illustration A.)** Your measurements may vary—check your printer owner's manual for paper margin information.

2. In your drawing or layout program, set up guidelines for the grid, as explained in step I. Determine where your photo should sit within that grid.

3. In your image-editing software, open an image of a face. Proportion the image to fit your stamp. Adjust the coloring and make any other corrections you want, such as removing the background and replacing it with colors or patterns. Save this in a format that you can import into your drawing or layout program.

4. Place your photo image in the first stamp. Using your text tool, add a stamp denomination or other text. **(See Illustration B.)** Select the photo and text and group them. Copy and paste this grouped

image into each successive space, until the grid is full.

5. Print your images on self-adhesive paper. This type of paper may dry more slowly than plain bond and will be more susceptible to smudging if it is still wet, so be sure to allow it to dry thoroughly.

6. To facilitate peeling the backing off the stamps after they have been trimmed out, *lightly* score the back of the self-adhesive sheet with a craft knife before they are trimmed. (Don't cut through the stamps!)

7. Using decorative-edge scissors, cut the pieces apart. **(See Illustration C.)** Now you're ready to use the stamps!

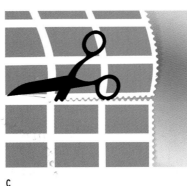

C

Creativity

• Design stamps in different sizes and shapes: squares, rectangles, triangles. For a layout of triangular stamps, set up a grid of rectangles, then add diagonal lines to divide the rectangles into triangles. Create your image and text, copy it all, rotate it 45 degrees, and paste it into the subsequent triangle. Continue to alternate upright and reversed images.

• These stamps make great collage materials. Take them a step farther by laminating them, adding a pin back, and wearing them with a favorite outfit.

IDENTITY PACKAGE

Every company has one—shouldn't you? Whether for personal or business purposes, it's a great idea to create an identity to present yourself on paper to others. For individuals this can be as simple as personalized stationery or as fun as creating "trading cards" with the particulars you want everyone to know. Kids can even make these and swap them with friends at school!

Get ready to create a complete identity system by using one central image or logo and arranging the information in a variety of ways. Our complete stationery package consists of letterhead, envelopes, fax cover sheets, mailing labels, business cards, notepads, and notecards. We will show you how to use the same motif on all the pieces so you have a consistent presentation.

What You'll Need

MATERIALS
Selected paper (writing stock, envelopes, label stock, card stock, scrap paper)
Aleene's Tacky Glue™ or other white glue
Cardboard for backing the notepads

TOOLS
Craft knife
Rotary cutter or paper cutter
Straightedge
Self-healing cutting mat
Wide rubber bands
Scrap cardboard or wood
2 C-Clamps
1-inch-wide disposable sponge paintbrush

ART
Clip art, decorative fonts

SOFTWARE
Drawing and page-layout programs

SKILL LEVEL
Intermediate

COMPLETION TIME
Logo: 2 hours
Letterhead: 1½ hours
Envelopes: ½ hour
Fax cover sheet: 1 hour
Mailing labels: ½ hour
Business cards: 1 hour
Personalized notepads: 3 hours
Notecards: ½ hour

Logo

Your logo is a graphic device that summarizes who you are and what you represent. There are two elements: type treatment and design. Select colors and type styles that best say "you." For instance, serif designs are more formal while san serif designs are usually breezier. Consider using a photographic image to add a more contemporary touch. Look for puns, memorable items, and other eye-catchers to set your image apart.

1. Make a rough sketch of your layout. This will allow you to play with the position of the elements in "sketch mode." Scan in the elements you have decided to use. Insert these images in your drawing or painting document and arrange them according to your sketch. Play with the proportions and relationships of the objects, and add any necessary copy, names, or the like. (See our examples in **Illustration A.)** When you have what you want, save this document as "Logo" in a suitable format for your software.

2. Print the logo on a variety of papers to test the color balance and how well it sizes—make it twice as big and then half as big to see what happens to details. Now the fun starts!

A

Letterhead

Some stationery stores sell paper by the pound, and paper speciality stores often sell larger quantities of a wide selection of papers. When you select your paper stock, remember that your letterhead may be used for various purposes, some more serious than others. Some of the fun choices sporting balloons or confetti may not be appropriate for business letters. Being your own printer enables you to tailor each letter to the recipient and the purpose.

1. Open your page-layout software and create an $8^1/_2$- x 11-inch page. Calculate space for your printer margins and decide where to place the logo. Choose the upper left for a traditional look, or opt for a more casual alternative by placing the logo in the center of the page or even at the bottom. **(See Illustration B.)** As you experiment, consider balance and where the text of the letter will be placed.

2. Add the necessary text—your street address, mailing address, phone numbers, fax numbers, URLs, and other contact information. Style and size the text to coordinate with your logo, and align it on the page. When you have arranged it the way you want, save the document as a template (see page 32). Run tests with a letter typed in to make sure it all works for you.

3. Print this document on writing stock, to be used as letterhead when you need a letter, in which case you'll be sending the preprinted paper back through the printer. Or, for each new letter, you can open your template, save it as a new letter document, type your letter, and print it on your selected blank paper.

B

C

Envelopes

This can be adapted to many other envelope sizes—just about anything that can be fed into your printer.

1. Create a document for your #10 business-sized envelope, $9^1/_2$ x $4^1/_8$ inches, referring to your printer's envelope-handling specifications. We created ours so it appears on the screen in the same orientation as the envelope is fed into the printer. **(See Illustration C.)**

2. Place the logo and return address information well within the printer's margins.

3. Run a test and make any needed adjustments. Save this as your master envelope template. Whenever you need it, just type in the addressee information and print.

Fax Cover Sheet

You can easily turn your letterhead into a fax cover sheet. You may be able to insert fields that will be automatically filled in from the faxing software—items like the name and phone number of the addressee. Adapt a layout that you can preprint in multiples, to keep on hand and fill in manually when needed.

1. Assess your letterhead layout and make any changes necessary to suit the faxing requirements. Screens, tones, and photo images generally don't fax very well, so make any changes to eliminate those elements. Vertical lines aren't very practical either. Add any necessary fax-specific information (date, sender, recipient, company, number of pages sent).

2. Check your work by printing samples. Fax a test document to check alignment and tones.

Mailing Labels

Mailing labels can be created any size and shape you want, printed on $8^{1}/_{2}$- x 11-inch self-adhesive label stock, and hand-trimmed. Or you can use any prescored label stock, adapting your design to the provided template. We chose the former technique, but the choice is yours!

1. Study the instructions included with your labels. Open your page-layout software and set up the first label, following the manufacturer's template.

2. Arrange your logo, company name, return address, and any desired graphic elements. When you are satisfied with the placement, group the elements, then copy and paste the completed label into the template as many times as needed. **(See Illustration D.)**

3. Print a sample page in draft mode. Check for alignment.

4. Print as many pieces as you need. Save the document as a template and file for future use.

D

Tip

Keep some blanks on hand for occasional use, or use your template to insert a mailing list when you have a big mailing to do.

Business Cards

Stationery stores carry a wealth of supplies for inkjet printers, including perforated or die-cut stock made expressly for business cards. You can quickly apply your logo to this media. There are even preprinted background designs and textures to liven up your materials.

1. Study the instructions included with your business card stock. Open your page-layout software and arrange your logo and text for the first card, following the manufacturer's template.

2. Copy and paste the completed card into the template as many times as needed. **(See Illustration E.)**

3. When the template is filled, print a sample page to check for placement. When you are happy with the results, print as many pieces as you need on the business card stock. Save the document as a template, and file for future use.

4. Separate the business cards along the laser perforations. You're ready to attend that convention!

Tip

Working with your own layout allows you a much wider choice of papers. Just remember that if you are printing on your own card stock and hand trimming, you will need to add trim marks to the layout for every cut (even a little dot will suffice) so you can see where to trim. Place them in the margins so they don't show after cutting.

E

Personalized Notepads

Here's a project that takes a bit more time but is so much fun, you'll love doing it! This is also a great way to recycle papers—any paper that has one clean, blank side can be used. About 50 sheets of plain bond make a $^1/_4$-inch-thick pad. Grocery-type list blanks can fit sideways, three to a page. Scoring pads for games or phone message pads may look better in quarter-page format.

Aleene's Tacky Glue™ is the best "padding" glue but good-quality white glue or yellow carpenter's glue also works quite well. If you don't have C-clamps, use a brick or two, a heavy weight, or a heavy can from your pantry, but remember that heavier is better: the tighter the packs are held together during the gluing process, the less the paper will warp as it absorbs moisture during this stage.

An $8^1/_2$- x 11-inch sheet can easily be divided into four pieces, yielding pads measuring $4^1/_4$ x $5^1/_2$ inches. Our instructions refer to these dimensions. We used the same elements as on our letterhead, adjusting the copy a bit.

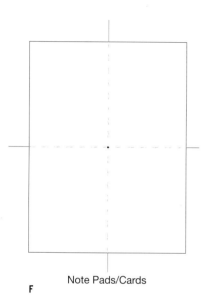

Note Pads/Cards

F

1. Open your graphics program and draw guidelines. **(See Illustration F.)** The dotted lines are guides for placement of the art; they do not print. If necessary, place a very small dot in the center to aid in trimming.

2. Place your logo and add the desired text. If you want a pad with ruled lines, draw several straight horizontal lines that start and stop about $^1/_4$ inch from each side.

3. When you are satisfied with the placement, group the elements, then copy and paste the design into the remaining three quadrants. Check your positioning. You now have a complete layout for the notepad.

4. Print 50 sheets. If you are using recycled paper that has already been used on one side (a good use for test pages!), make sure to follow your printer directions to place the paper in the loading tray correctly.

5. Set the pages aside to dry for about an hour to allow them to absorb the ink completely.

6. Cut the pads to size following your guidelines, using a paper cutter. You can also use a craft knife or rotary cutter and a straightedge on a padded surface. Several sheets may be cut at the same time by holding your straightedge firmly to prevent slipping.

7. Prepare your work area in a spot where you can leave the notepad to dry undisturbed for several hours. You'll be clamping the notepad stacks to the edge of a table or workbench, so choose a surface that is firm enough to support a two-inch stack of material and a C-clamp. Test to make sure your C-clamp is wide enough to accommodate the table and the paper stack. Protect the surface and the edge with scrap paper. Remember to put lots of newspaper on the floor to catch glue drips.

8. Trim cardboard sheets to fit the dimensions of your notepad, preparing one cardboard backing piece per notepad.

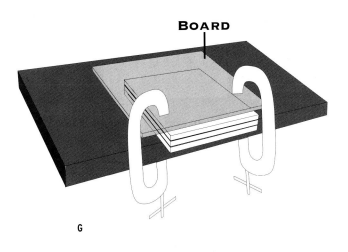

BOARD

G

9. Arrange your cut paper sheets into stacks about $1/4$ inch thick, generally about 50 pages. Place a cardboard backing sheet under each stack. Stack the notepads in piles, up to eight pads in a pile. Use wide rubber bands to keep the piles in place.

10. Align the spines (edges to be bound), extending the stack slightly off the edge of the work surface so it can be clamped. Put a few pieces of stiff cardboard or a scrap of wood on top, aligned with

the spine edge. Clamp this to the work surface with two C-clamps. **(See Illustration G.)**

11. With a disposable paintbrush, spread an even, moderately thick layer of glue over the spine. Allow to dry for several hours, according to the glue manufacturer's directions. Carpenter's glue needs just one coat, but white glues and tacky glue will require a second layer.

12. When the stack is thoroughly dry, carefully separate the pads with a craft knife.

Tip

A copy shop can trim and pad your printed, untrimmed sheets for you, but with just a little practice you can get quite good at doing this yourself.

Creativity

You can adapt these notepads endlessly. Personalized with the recipient's name, they make great gifts. Create specific pads for games like bridge. Or give them different headings to use as shopping or to-do lists.

Notecards

1. Use the notepad template to lay out your design so you can fit four on a page, each $5^1/2$ x $4^1/4$inches. They can be very simple, with just your name and logo, or you can add more contact information. When you are satisfied with the placement, group the elements, then copy and paste the design into the remaining three quadrants. Check your positioning.

2. Print the notecards on card stock. Trim them and they are ready for quick postcard notes or reminders. They can also be used with standard A-2 announcement envelopes found at paper supply stores.

CHAPTER THREE

holiday and gift ideas

WOVEN BASKET

Here is a simple, quick, fun project that can be used in the office or home, or for parties and other special occasions. With their colorful graphics, these baskets make a charming statement. The idea is to cover a page with lots of color, designs, and text, then cut the pages into strips and weave them together. You can also add a handle. The beefier the paper, the longer your basket will last.

What You'll Need

MATERIALS
Card stock
Self-adhesive paper, 8 ½ x 11 inches

TOOLS
Bone folder
Straightedge
Craft knife
Low-tack tape
Double-sided tape

ART
Scanned images, computer graphics, or clip art

SOFTWARE
Image-editing or drawing program

SKILL LEVEL
Easy

COMPLETION TIME
1 hour

1. In a drawing program or image-editing program, cover an $8^1/_2$- x 11-inch area with a variety of designs, text, images, and color. To create our design, we scanned a collage of Victorian images from clip art books and other sources, positioning them so that each image overlapped several others. Try moving your images around, rotating them, and changing their scale.

2. Make a second page of designs using different colors, images, or another form of contrast. Save both pages. Print them on your chosen paper. Print one of the designs again on $8^1/_2$- x 11-inch self-adhesive paper. You are printing two different pages to weave, then printing one again on the adhesive paper, which will become the finishing trim. You will have some printed adhesive paper left over to trim other boxes.

3. Score the fold lines; each score line should be 2 inches away from the center, which will make the basket bottom 4 inches square. **(See Illustration A.)** With a craft knife and straightedge, cut each of the two card-stock sheets into $3/4$-inch-wide strips. You will need nine strips for the basket, plus five for weaving in one side, four for the second side, and one for the handle. Leave the last $1/4$-inch of nine of the strips uncut to aid in assembly. Be sure to eliminate the white, unprinted area along the two long edges, as shown. (The remaining two unprinted margins will be covered by the self-adhesive trimming after the box is built.) Gently fold the strips on the scored lines, then let them relax.

4. Place the set of nine connected strips face down on a flat surface. Lightly tape the connected side to the surface with low-tack tape to help keep the strips in place while weaving.

5. Weave five fully cut strips face down through the taped-down strips, positioning them across the center. **(See Illustration B.)** You may want to tape down the finished ends with low-tack tape during assembly. Remove the tape when weaving is complete.

(continued on next page)

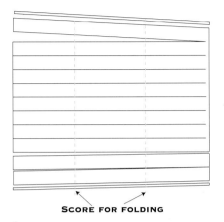

SCORE FOR FOLDING

A

Tip

• With a little advanced planning, you can place letters to form a message on your box. Remember that alternating areas along a strip will be covered by the weaving pattern, so place each character one strip-width away from the last. Weave this one face up to ensure it's laid out correctly.

• You can use wider or narrower strips and longer paper. The proportions of the box can be changed by altering the dimensions of the bottom.

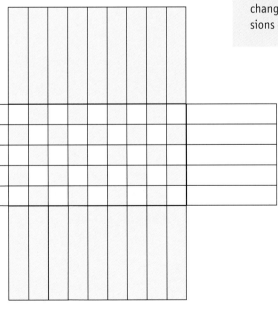

B

Creativity

• Another way to approach this is to make the equivalent of ikat dyeing. Print two sheets exactly the same and interweave them. The design will be reformed in its entirety with some slight variations where the paper is woven and folded. Try one of these with narrower strips for an intriguing look.

• The potential for Easter baskets is obvious, but also think about making one for your office to hold business cards or paper clips.

• Use all sorts of filling. Try shredding used paper very finely, or choose moss for a realistic look. Craft stores often sell shredded metallic paper, which would add some real pizzazz. Or opt for cellophane bags in pretty pastel colors, which are readily available at Easter time but may also be available year-round in the craft store.

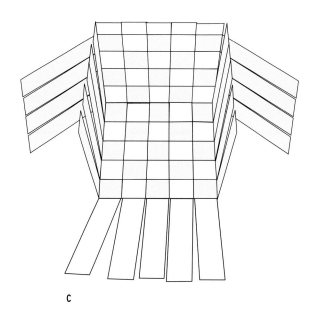

C

6. Fold up one side on the score line, which will make the basket side four strips high. **(See Illustration C.)** Weave unwoven ends of the four strips into the five from the base to create the second side. Repeat this on the opposite side. You now have a three-sided box.

7. Fold up the remaining side and weave in four additional strips **(See Illustration D.)** Weave them back into the two adjoining sides, trimming the ends that extend too far after they have been tucked in. Now your box has been formed. Trim the ends around the top with scissors to even them up.

8. To finish off the basket, cut the self-adhesive paper into 3/4-inch-wide strips and wrap the top edge of the box, overlapping the ends of the strips.

9. If you wish, attach a handle. Prefold the handle so that it forms a gentle arch. **(See Illustration E.)** Slide the ends into the weaving of the basket below the self-adhesive trim, fold up the extending piece, and tape to secure. Fill and have fun!

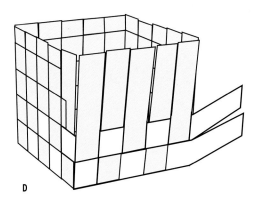

D

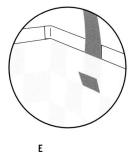

E

SIX-SIDED BOX

A beautiful, personalized gift box; a color-coded, labeled container to store precious objects—you can adapt this box endlessly to suit any occasion. Once you create one box, you will be busy filling orders for the entire family. The decorating possibilities are unlimited: with color, with patterns, with type, with scanned images, you'll enjoy using the decorations that you love.

For our birthday box we used three tones of blue, alternating patterns of stripes, dots, and stars with names written against a plain blue ground. The star pattern is available in many drawing programs.

What You'll Need

MATERIALS
Cover-weight (65–80 lb.) paper or tag board, 8½ x 11 inches

TOOLS
Craft knife
Straightedge
Self-healing cutting mat
Bone folder
Double-sided tape, white glue, or rubber cement

ART
Scanned images, computer graphics, clip art, decorative fonts

SOFTWARE
Drawing or painting program

SKILL LEVEL
Intermediate

COMPLETION TIME
1½ to 2 hours

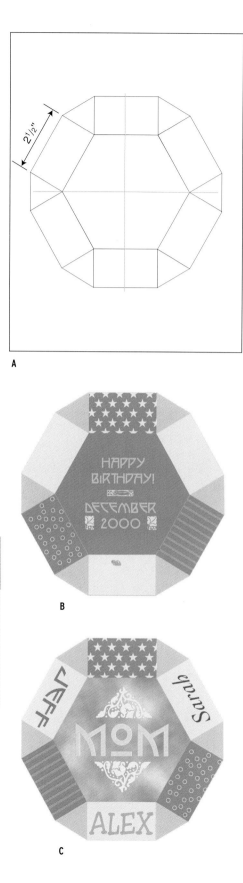

A

B

C

1. For the bottom of the box, create a hexagon measuring $2\frac{1}{2}$ inches per side and center it on your page. Create a rectangle measuring $2\frac{1}{2}$ inches by $1\frac{1}{2}$ inches. Place the rectangle along the top side of the hexagon. Duplicate this rectangle, rotate it 60 degrees, and place it along the next side. Repeat these steps until you have a rectangle along all six sides. Connect the outer corners of the rectangles, forming $1\frac{1}{2}$-inch equilateral triangles, to make the tabs. This is the basic box structure. **(See Illustration A.)**

2. Fill the areas with the colors and patterns you have chosen. Add text if you want. You may want to "bleed" the color or shapes past the edges of your box to ensure complete coverage, but be careful to keep images within the trim markings. When you are satisfied with the layout, group the art. **(See Illustration B.)**

3. To make the top, copy the box bottom pattern and enlarge it to 102 percent of the original size to allow it to fit comfortably over the bottom. Adjust the patterns, images, and text as necessary; keep in mind that if you want the patterns on the sides to match when the finished box is closed, you must transpose the positioning. (Compare the location of the striped and dotted sides on Illustrations B and C.) For the top of our birthday box, we made the sides $1\frac{3}{8}$ inches deep, so the box bottom is fully covered when the box is closed. **(See Illustration C.)** For our memory box, we made the sides $\frac{1}{2}$ inch deep so the sides of the box bottom are partially visible when the lid is on. **(See Illustration D.)**

D

4. Print the top and bottom on cover-weight paper or tag board. Allow the sheets to dry flat on a surface for about a half hour to ensure the inks have been fully absorbed.

5. With a craft knife and straight-edge, trim the box around the outside edge. Create the tabs by cutting from A to B only on the left side of the rectangles **(See Illustration E.)** Score all the folds (around the central hexagon and along the tab edges) and crease

them well with the bone folder so they will hold a nice sharp edge when the tabs are glued.

6. Tuck the tabs behind the sides, aligning the edges carefully, and adhere them in place with double-sided tape, white glue, or rubber cement. **(See Illustration F.)** Let the box dry overnight if you used white glue, or several hours for rubber cement.

Creativity

• Make a souvenir box by scanning a panoramic photo from a trip. Scale and divide it appropriately into rectangles. Rotate and place them into position on your pattern to create the sides.

• Try a quotation box. Find an appropriate quote—one with six words is ideal—and type in each word or small group of words on one of the rectangles. Size the longest word or word grouping to 2⅜ inches wide, then match the remainder of the words to that point size.

• You might want to put your name and date or a message across the top or bottom of the lid, as we did on the birthday box. Some brands of printers allow you to print on both sides of cover stock, which opens up lots of possibilities for secret messages or hidden pictures!

CUT
FOLD - - - - - -

A
B

E

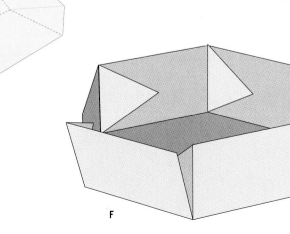

F

PARTY FAVOR BAG

Here is a quick project that can be used in many ways. Put in some pretty colored shredded paper and a few candies as a goody bag for children's parties. Make one with your logo printed on it and use it to hold office supplies on your desk at work. This is a perfect promotional item—print them with directions for assembly and send them to clients.

1. Orient your page and paper to landscape mode. Draw a rectangle $10^1/_2$ inches long and $3^1/_2$ inches high. Fill it with color. Set the stroke to "none." Set guidelines at, from the left side, $3^1/_2$ inches, 5 inches, $8^1/_2$ inches, and 10 inches. **(See Illustration A.)**

2. Create a rectangle $3^1/_2$ inches wide by $1^1/_2$ inches high. Make sure that the attributes are set to fill the box with color and to put no stroke on it. Move it to touch the bottom of the third division formed in the previous step; this is the bottom of the bag, as shown.

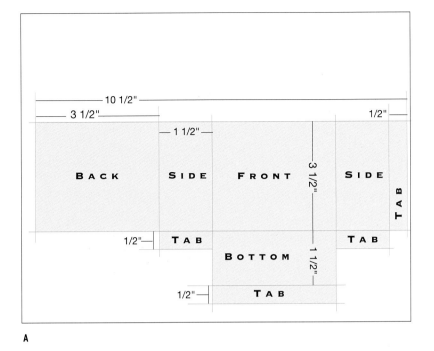

10 1/2"

3 1/2"   1/2"

1 1/2"

BACK   **SIDE**   **FRONT**   3 1/2"   **SIDE**   **T A B**

1/2"   **TAB**

BOTTOM   1 1/2"   **TAB**

1/2"   **TAB**

A

3. Draw a rectangle $1^1/_2$ inches wide by $^1/_2$ inch high. Make sure it is filled with color and has no stroke. Place it on one side of the bottom. Copy and paste a second one on the other side. Create a third rectangle, $1^1/_2$ inches by $^1/_2$ inch, and place it beneath the bottom. These three narrow rectangles, together with the one formed at the far right, are the glue tabs, as shown. Group all the rectangles together.

4. To indicate the fold lines, draw lines with your pen tool, utilizing your software's capabilities to draw a perfectly straight horizontal or vertical line—usually this is done by holding down the shift key while you draw. The lines should be either $^1/_2$ or 1 point wide and stroked a shade or two darker than the base color. Place these lines using your guidelines. **(See Illustration B.)**

(continued on next page)

Creativity

• Depending on your occasion, you can go from conservative to hog-wild on this project. Personalize each gift bag for a party with the person's name or photograph. Decorate the handles to give a 3-D appearance by adding clip art or photographs. Make sure the type complements the design of the bag so the entire object is pleasing to the eye.

• Consider using this as a place to put the buttons that come with new clothes: create a button design with a couple of concentric circles and four dots for the thread holes. Keep it in your closet and drop the funny little bag that comes with your new blouse right into your holder—you'll always know where to find it!

• There will be some leftover white space on your project page. Use that margin creatively—for example, make a gift tag that fits the empty space. If you are sending this to someone in its flat form, include assembly instructions in the white margins.

B

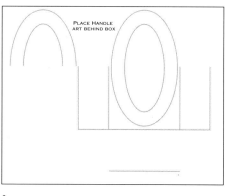

PLACE HANDLE
ART BEHIND BOX

C

Morgan

D

5. To make the handles, use your ellipse tool to draw an oval 3^1/$_4$ inches wide and 5^1/$_2$ inches high. Draw a second one 2 inches wide and 4^1/$_8$ inches high. Align the two ovals by positioning their center points to coincide. Group them, then copy and paste them. (They will be positioned in the next step.) Stroke the lines with color if needed as a guide for cutting. Center one handle on one side, with the top of the handle about ^{1}/$_2$ inch from the top of the page. Place the second handle similarly on the second side. Send both to the back layer. **(See Illustration C;** note that the right handle is shown before it is put in position behind the other elements.)

6. Now for the really fun part: creating a design. The directions here explain how we did ours **(see Illustration D)**, but you can make your own designs as desired. Using our brush tool, with the brush stroke set to none and the fill set to a color, we first drew a freehand blue box in the area bounded by the top of the bag, the fold lines, and the left margin. Then, with the ellipse tool, we drew an orange circle in the middle of the box and placed a circle filled with yellow behind it. With the brush tool again we drew a series of red zigzag lines, creating a sunburst shape. We copied the design and pasted it on the other side of the bag. For the side, we used the brush tool to draw another freehand blue box and a red zigzag line from top to bottom. For the handle, we drew a small box with an orange brush line. With the box tool, we drew a box the same size filled with yellow and placed it behind the orange one. We positioned these two elements at the base of one end of the handle. We copied and pasted these two boxes to the other end of the handle. We then drew two waving lines to connect the two boxes. We then grouped, copied, and pasted them on the second handle.

7. Print your bag on cover-weight paper. With a craft knife, cut out along the outer edges. Score, fold, and crease on the fold lines. Assemble the box, adhering the tabs with rubber cement, white glue, or double-sided tape. **(See Illustration E.)** If you are using glue, let the bag dry a few hours.

E

GIFT BOX

Card stock paper can greatly extend the range of projects you can create with your color printer. For example, here is a simple box you can build, using a quick template. There are two ways to approach this. You can print the designs directly on the card stock, or you can print them on your highest-quality paper and then glue the paper onto card stock with spray adhesive. This makes a firm layer and allows for output on a higher-quality surface.

What You'll Need

MATERIALS
Card stock, 8½ x 11 inches
Good-quality paper (optional)

TOOLS
Craft knife
Straightedge
Self-healing cutting mat
Bone folder
Spray varnish
Double-sided tape, or tacky glue
   for heavier-weight papers

ART
Scanned images, clip art,
   decorative fonts

SOFTWARE
Drawing program

SKILL LEVEL
Easy

COMPLETION TIME
1 hour

1. Construct the template in a drawing program, following our layout. **(See Illustration A.)** The red dotted lines indicate fold lines; the black solid lines are the cutting lines. Draw a box 8½ x 3⅜ inches, then draw two boxes each 1⅜ inches wide by 3 inches tall, positioning one on each side of the tall rectangle, 1⅜ inches from the top edge. Using your line tool and starting at the top edge of the tall rectangle, place a point slightly (approximately ⅛ inch) lower than the top edge and 1⅛ inches to the left. The second point on the line is where this line intersects the left-hand box edge. Create three more tabs exactly like this and position them as indicated in the template. Add rounded flaps to the right and left sides, using the ellipse tool. Add one more flap at the bottom of the tall rectangle. Finally, add two horizontal fold lines, one 3 inches from the bottom of the tall rectangle, and one 1⅜ inches above that. Position the box within the printer margins.

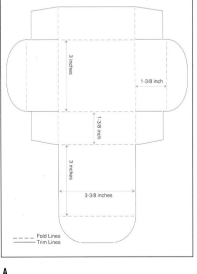

A

(continued on next page)

B

C

2. Using scanned material, clip art, or images painted or drawn in your software, decorate the surfaces of the box template. Some of the Photoshop effects we used were "Gaussian Blur," "Clouds," transparency, deckle, and erased edges. The text was added as a last step. **(See Illustrations B and C.)** Check your editing software for similar commands and capabilities, or test out others that seem interesting. If you can print on both sides of your paper, you can make both an inside and an outside design.

3. To create subtle cutting lines that won't show after you cut out the box, change the black and red lines to a color that is very close to the color of the box itself and make sure this template is the top layer.

4. Print the image on card stock, or on good paper if you are going to laminate it to heavier stock.

5. If you are printing on both sides, return the paper to the paper tray and print the other side. Before printing, double check that the paper is properly loaded!

6. Cut out the box along the solid lines. Score, fold, and crease along the fold lines. Using double-sided tape or tacky glue, adhere the tabs inside the box as shown. **(See Illustration D.)** Use a spray varnish on the outside of the box to make it a bit sturdier and long-lasting.

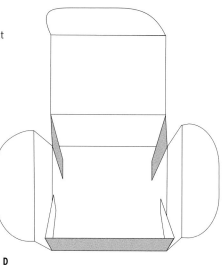

D

ORIGAMI BOX

Origami is the art of folding paper into amusing and sometimes useful objects. By cleverly placing images or type, our project produces a very personalized piece. This cute little box can be made from one $8^1/_2$- x 11-inch sheet of paper. The total image area is $7^1/_2$ inches square; the image area for the top of the box is $2^5/_8$ inches square. You can create an overall design to cover the whole box or, as we did, treat the top and sides individually. Duplicate our template so you can make these by the dozens, as a quick party favor, filled with a few candies, or as a present for a very special someone.

What You'll Need

MATERIALS
Good-quality paper

TOOLS
Craft knife
Straightedge
Self-healing cutting mat
Bone folder
Double-sided tape

ART
Scanned images, clip art,
   decorative fonts

SOFTWARE
Drawing program

SKILL LEVEL
Easy

COMPLETION TIME
½ hour

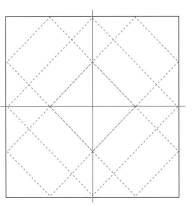

1. In your drawing program, create a box $5^1/_4$ inches square. Create another box $2^5/_8$ inches square. Center this second box in the middle of the larger box. Rotate these at a 45-degree angle and center them on your page. Now draw a third box, $7^1/_2$ inches square. Position this box to encase the two diamonds. Using your line tool, create center lines for both the horizontal and vertical axes. These are for positioning and will be deleted before printing. **(See Illustration A, part 1.)**

2. Draw a box $2^5/_8$ inches square. Rotate the box by 45 degrees. Copy and paste this box three times.

   (continued on next page)

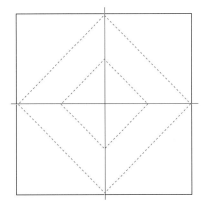

A

Creativity

These can be used as party favors, business gimmicks, or rainy day activities for kids. Help children personalize the boxes with their names and art they have created, or gear the boxes to a holiday theme, as in our Halloween design.

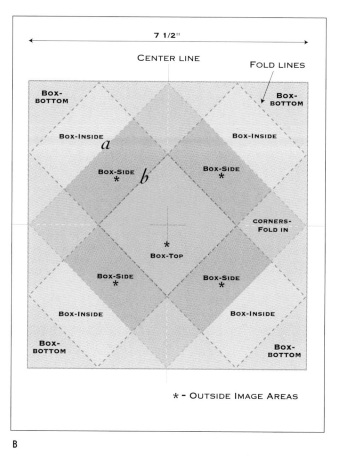

B

C

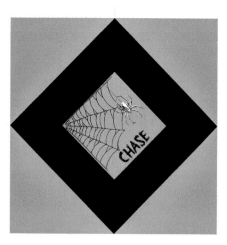

D

3. Position the first of these boxes along the top left edge of the inner diamond. This box will be bisected by the 5¹/₄-inch square. Position the next of these boxes along the upper right edge of the inner diamond. Place the third box along the lower right edge, and the final box along the lower left edge. You now have a template. **(See Illustrations A, part 2, and B.)**

4. Center your main image in the central diamond, rotated 45 degrees so it will appear straight and not on the diagonal once the box is folded. **(See Illustration C.)** If desired, place text on the four sections around the central image. **(See Illustration D.)**

Remember to allow for your unprintable paper margins. In addition to the top and sides, you can plan a design for the inside portion of the box. Our Halloween image was centered on the top of the box, then we created a black box to print on the four sides, and put orange on the four tabs that become the inside surfaces of the box.

5. Delete the horizontal and vertical axis lines that were created in step 1. Change the remaining fold lines to a color close in tone to the artwork and make sure the template is on top of the artwork so that you will have fold lines when printed.

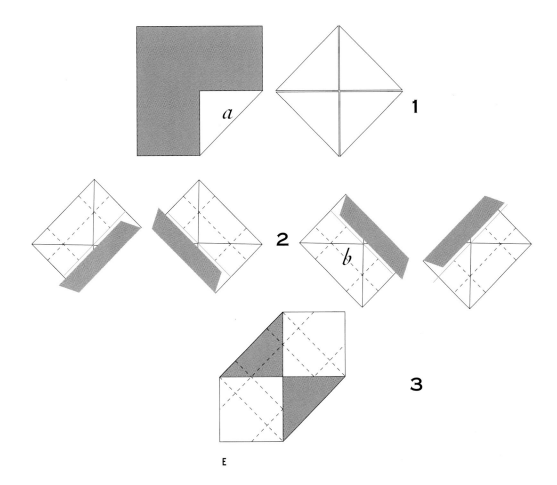

E

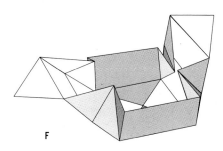

6. Print as many boxes as you need.

7. Cut your paper into an exact $7^1/2$- x $7^1/2$-inch square. Score along the dotted fold lines. Fold on lines A first, bringing all four corners into the center point, with the design on the outside. **(See Illustration E, part 1.)** Crease the folds on lines B, reopening each fold after creasing. **(See Illustration E, part 2.)** Open up the two corners marked by a red dot in our illustration. Secure the remaining two corners by placing a piece of double-sided tape in the center underneath them. **(See Illustration E, part 3.)**

8. Starting at one of the long pointed ends, fold the box corners down and inward. **(See Illustration F.)** Fold the flap over the tucked-in corners and push down into the inside of the box, securing the tip in the center on the tape. Repeat this with the other flap.

9. To make the bottom, cut the paper $^1/4$ inch smaller in each direction than the top piece so it will be slightly smaller and will thus allow the cover to slide over the bottom.

F

LUMINARIA

The Southwest has a holiday tradition of setting up luminaria to shine on a path during the Christmas season. These are traditionally made of paper bags with a candle set inside. Now you can improve on the technique using your computer and start a new tradition at your house! Make about twenty of them to line a walkway or driveway before a party to welcome guests with a cheerful glow. You can substitute small cheap flashlights for the riskier candles, but remember that these are "fair weather" decorations that must be saved for clear-sky times, and should never be used with a candle indoors.

The triangular design gives you three image areas, so browse through your collections of photos, art, and the like to come up with a pleasing trio of visuals. We used clip art and a photo of a niece, then drew some freehand lines as further embellishment. Experiment with your software to find interesting effects. Many types of paper will work, but if you use a lightweight type such as rice paper, place a triangle of cardboard in the bottom of the luminaria to add stability.

What You'll Need

MATERIALS
Legal-size plain bond paper or
  other paper of choice
Sand or kitty litter
Candles or flashlights

TOOLS
Craft knife
Straightedge
Self-healing cutting mat
Bone folder
Double-sided tape or white glue

ART
Clip art, scanned photographs

SOFTWARE
Drawing program

SKILL LEVEL
Intermediate

COMPLETION TIME
1 hour

1. In your drawing program, create a 14- x 8$^1/_2$-inch box. Draw a line across the page 4$^1/_2$ inches from the top edge. Draw three vertical lines from the top edge to this median line, positioning the first one 4$^1/_2$ inches from the left edge, the second 4$^1/_2$ inches to the right of the first, and the third 4$^1/_2$ inches to the right of the second. The narrow strip formed to the right of the third vertical is a tab for assembly. **(See Illustration A.)**

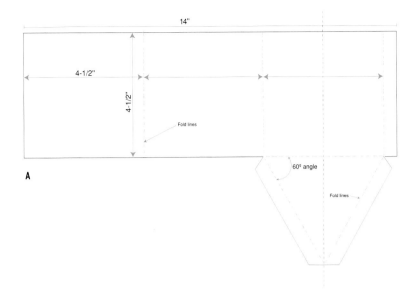

14"

4-1/2"

4-1/2"

Fold lines

60° angle

Fold lines

A

Creativity

- Give your luminaria a sculpted look by drawing shapes like the moon, the sun, and stars on them and cutting out only about half of the shape. Fold the cut areas slightly to the inside to let the light shine through more brightly.

- For a party, arrange some curbside luminaria that spell out your address. At holidays, decorate them with appropriate clip art. Or try making each luminaria a different color and then line them up like a rainbow.

- For a business party, enlarge your company's logo (simplifying it if necessary) to adorn your luminaria. Or put one huge letter on each luminaria to spell out your marketing slogan in a bold, bright fashion.

- You can also adapt this to use with Christmas tree lights. Before closing up the bottom flaps, thread the lights through, one bulb per luminaria. Place the lumaria carefully so that no one will trip over the wire, and be sure to use indoor/outdoor lights. You can also design these to be hung upside down from trees for a pool party, or string them through the branches of your bushes for late summer fun when dining alfresco.

2. Place an equilateral triangle on the lower right side of the page, aligning one edge along the base of the right-hand box, as shown. (NOTE: By default, drawing programs always draw equilateral triangles.) Add two tabs, one on each side as shown, for gluing in the assembly phase.

3. Size and place your chosen images, one in the center of each box. **(See Illustration B.)**

4. Print as many copies as needed on your selected paper.

5. Cut out the luminaria. Score and fold along each fold line. Adhere the tabs on the inside with double-sided tape or white glue. Begin with the side panels, then insert the tabs on the bottom triangle into the column. **(See Illustration C.)** If you use glue, allow it to dry thoroughly.

6. Put the luminaria in place outdoors. Pour a cupful of sand or kitty litter (clean, of course) into the bottom for stability. If you are using candles, stick the candle into the sand, which will act as a base to hold it upright. If using flashlights, place each one on top of this layer. Turn them on and watch your outdoor scene light up!

B

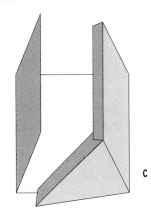

C

HALLOWEEN MASK

What You'll Need

MATERIALS
High-quality paper, 8½ x 11 inches
¼-inch-wide elastic, 12 inches per mask, or narrow ribbon, 24 inches per mask

TOOLS
Craft knife
Self-healing cutting mat
Hole punch

ART
Drawn images

SOFTWARE
Drawing or painting program

SKILL LEVEL
Intermediate

COMPLETION TIME
1 hour

Simple is good, especially when you are in a hurry and heading out to have some fun. This idea can be completed in minutes and really makes an impact. If you are going to a party, how much more fun to go as someone else—so sit right down at your computer and make yourself a mask. See ya at the party!

1. In your painting or drawing program, create a face that will fill up the entire page. Remember to include your printer margins in your calculations. For example, our printer's paper-handling system requires a ½-inch margin on each side, so we planned our face to be 10 inches high by 7½ inches wide. Place eye holes and a nose and mouth at the following approximate distances from the top edge of the face: eyes, 4½ inches; nose, 6½ inches; mouth, 7½ inches. **(See Illustration A.)**

2. To give the mask dimensionality and allow it to fit the curves of your face, create darts on each side by placing a point 1½ inches from each edge, slightly below the midpoint of the mask. Draw lines to form the sides of the dart that are about 1½ inches apart at their farthest point. Draw a small circle and place it just above the top line of the dart, as shown. Copy and paste the circle just above the bottom line of the dart. Repeat this on the other side.

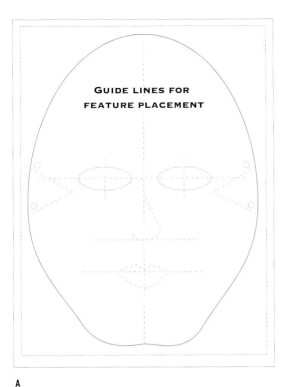

GUIDE LINES FOR
FEATURE PLACEMENT

A

B

3. Add the details of the facial features, hair, and decorative elements. **(See Illustration B.)** We drew these features using free-hand and ellipse tools, but you could also use clip art or scanned pieces of photographs. Note that we adjusted the hair placement on the woman's face to accommodate the dart. This was done by dupli-cating the triangle of hair that fell within the dart lines and rotating it, so the art will match when the dart is created. We tested the posi-tioning by printing out a copy and adjusting the art in our design. You may need to use this trial-and-error method as well.

4. Print the mask on your best paper and allow the ink to fully absorb before proceeding.

5. Cut out the mask along the outside edge. Cut out the eyeholes and the mouth opening and cut a slit for the nose. Cut along the upper edge of the dart and punch holes at the circles.

6. Bring the two holes together on each side, insert the elastic, and tie it off. **(See Illustration C.)** Tie off the other end of the elastic through the holes on the other side to complete the mask. If you prefer, use two 12-inch lengths of ribbon, one on each side of the mask.

C

Creativity

• Blow up a picture of a loved one, a celebrity, or a famous artwork for your mask. How about using Mona Lisa's face? Or go for a geometric look with an all-over pattern. Try photographs of circuit boards to make an android mask.

• Kids can make this project, since it requires little time and few materials. At a party, you could have each new arrival assemble a mask that sets the party theme in motion. Scan photos of animals, for instance, and have children put together a whole barnyard or zoo full of masks.

• Although these masks use plain paper, you could use heavier-weight card stock and embellish the mask with earrings, glitter, feathers, and other party materials.

CHAPTER FOUR

toys and games

PAPER AIRPLANE

You probably remember several paper airplane designs from elementary school. All of them are fun, and now you can add a new dimension by personalizing them and creating a level of realism, which was impossible before the advent of inexpensive color printers. Our classic pattern is shown with its fold lines and fun designs—all you have to do is re-create it in living color—what could be simpler? We give you a basic shape, but there are countless variations on this style, so once you've made this one, try your own designs!

What You'll Need

MATERIALS
High-quality paper, plain bond
   paper, or card stock, 8½ x 11
   inches
Paper clip (optional)

TOOLS
Craft knife
Self-healing cutting mat
Bone folder
Straightedge
Double-sided tape

ART
Drawn images, clip art,
   decorative fonts, dingbats

SOFTWARE
Drawing program

SKILL LEVEL
Easy

COMPLETION TIME
½ hour

1. Before you get started, check the maximum size of the printable area for your brand of printer (see "Paper handling," page 33).

2. In a drawing program, create a box 7½ inches wide by 10 inches long and center it in the middle of your page, making sure it fits completely within the printable area. Fill the box with peach color and use no stroke color.

3. Divide the box vertically in half to indicate your center fold line. Draw two more fold lines, each radiating from the center line at the top of the box to 3¾ inches from the top edge of your box for fold line A. **(See Illustration A.)** Draw two more lines, again radiating from the top center point, this time ending ¹³/₁₆ inch from the bottom edges of the box, for fold line B. For fold line C, draw two more lines running from a point 1½ inches from the top of line B to a point 1⁹/₁₆ inches from the center of the lower edge of the box. To indicate the underside of the wing, draw line D, beginning at the same point as line C and ending midway between lines A and B. For the tail section, draw line E as shown. You can now see which areas to decorate for the wing top, plane sides, and tail.

4. Decorate the aircraft with clip art, decorative fonts, and dingbats. We made ours for a birthday party and put the name of the birthday boy on the tail! **(See Illustration B.)**

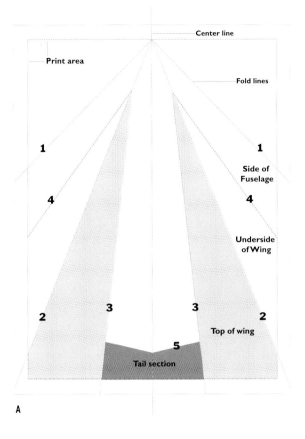

Center line

Print area

Fold lines

1   1

Side of
Fuselage

4   4

Underside
of Wing

     3   3

2   2

Top of wing

5

Tail section

A

B

5. Print your creation in either high-quality mode on special paper, or medium mode on plain bond paper or card stock.

6. Trim the white edges and score the fold lines. Now you're ready to fold. Follow **Illustration C** as your guide, and crease the folds sharply as you go. First, fold in half lengthwise along the center line, bringing the two printed sides together (see first step of illustration). We found it helpful to trim the tail (line E) at this time. Next, fold down along line A (second step) and then down again along lines B (third step) and then C (fourth step). Fold the tail section (fifth step) back up into the airplane so it will stick above the wings (sixth step).

7. Secure the folds with double-sided tape, and add a paper clip for ballast. You're ready to fly your plane!

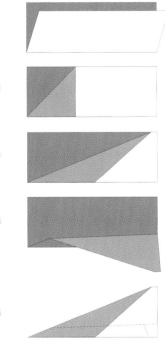

C

Creativity

• Send a message to someone special—written on the wings!

• Use colors for different looks—green for a fighter plane, blue for a high flyer, pink for a dainty craft, and so on. Decorations can suit the mood of the plane. For example, for that pink craft, use a row of hearts to decorate the main spine of the craft, then type "H. P. Lovecraft" on the sides in big purple letters, outlined with baby blue.

PUPPET

Have you seen those delightful Javanese puppets that are so colorful and exotic? A similar style of puppet is easy to make at home. The key to this project is to adapt the color scheme and style to create a similar look. We used an image from an old illustration of Punch. Then again, you can always make up your own style and characters for any sort of home performance. These also make great wall decor.

What You'll Need

MATERIALS
Card stock, or plain paper and
   thin cardboard
8 brass paper fasteners
5 thin dowels or wooden strips,
   18 inches each
Ribbon (optional)

TOOLS
Scissors
Craft knife
Self-healing cutting mat
Hole punch
White glue
Spray adhesive (optional)

ART
Scanned or drawn images

SOFTWARE
Painting and/or drawing
   program

SKILL LEVEL
Intermediate

COMPLETION TIME
2 hours

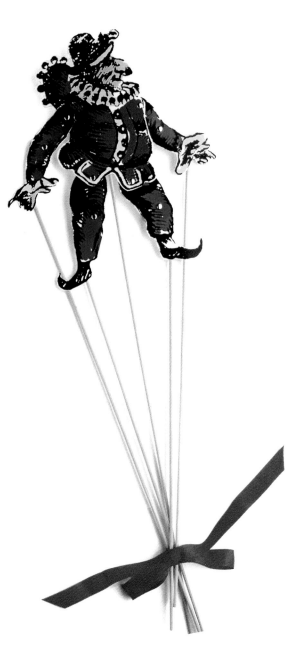

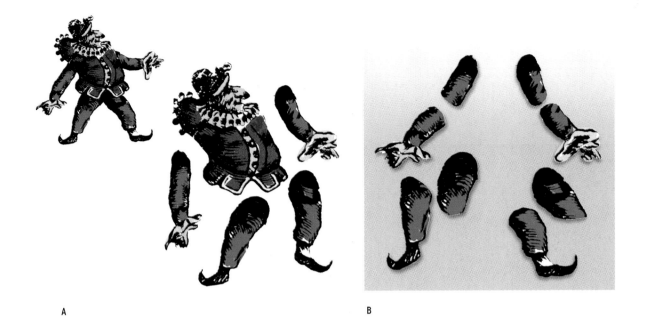

A   B

1. You will create three pages—one for the head/body, one for the legs, and one for the arms. **(See Illustration A.)** If you are creating your own figure, start with the head and body. Draw the shape of a head; include hats, ears, and other design elements as you wish. Using drawing or painting tools, decorate the head. Choose a color palette that is appropriate to your project. (The Indonesians used a lot of browns and dark blues with strong reds on off-white backgrounds, but use colors to suit your own design.) Add a body to the head. Make the neck fairly substantial so that it does not bend or droop.

2. In order to form an overlapping area where each limb will join the body, we selected the first limb, then copied and pasted it into a new document. Using drawing tools and colors from our image, we shaped an extension to the top of the arm. This was to be placed behind the body when we assembled the puppet, so it needed to look similar to the rest of the arm. **(See Illustration B.)**

3. Repeat for the remaining limbs. Return to the torso and neatly remove the limbs, leaving a complete image, as shown.

4. In order to create the overlap needed to make the elbow joint, duplicate the arm. On one of the images, erase the top half, leaving a section above the elbow for the overlap. On the second arm, erase the bottom half, leaving a section below the elbow for the overlap. (This will allow room to punch holes later to articulate the joint.) Repeat this for the remaining limbs.

5. Print your images on card stock or other firm paper. If you do not have card stock, print on regular paper and then glue to a sheet of cardboard.

6. You can make your puppet two-sided by printing a second set with the images reversed for the back of the puppet. Or, if your equipment allows, print on both sides, but be sure to align your elements very carefully so that they will print accurately.

(continued on next page)

C

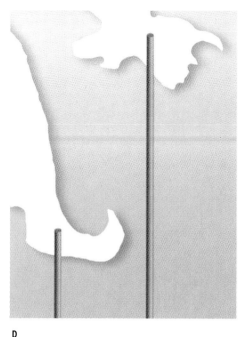

D

Creativity

• Make this into a marionette by attaching string to each piece and connecting the strings to a dowel or a piece of wire.

• The image choices are endless. You could make your whole family into puppets by scanning full-length photos, then using image-editing software to cut and paste the pieces to form the separate arms, legs, and body. Or make animal puppets using images from children's books.

7. Cut out the pieces with scissors if using card stock. If using plain paper, first glue it to the cardboard with spray adhesive or white glue and let dry thoroughly, then cut the pieces with a craft knife. For a two-sided puppet printed on separate pages, cut the pieces and glue them to the back of the original set. If using regular paper and cardboard, glue the paper of the reversed pieces directly to the cardboard that is backing the front pieces; you don't need two layers of cardboard.

8. Align the upper and lower limbs and the body and punch holes for the paper fasteners at the shoulders, elbows, upper thighs, and knees. Connect the pieces with paper fasteners. **(See Illustration C.)**

9. Glue the dowels to the back with white glue, placing one behind the body and one at each limb. **(See Illustration D.)** When the glue is thoroughly dry, trim the dowels with a craft knife as necessary so they align at the bottom.

10. To operate the puppet, hold the main dowel and move the arm and leg pieces up and down with the dowels

11. To make an attractive decorative accent out of your puppet, tie the dowels together at the base with a nice bow, attach a ribbon to the back of the puppet's head, and hang on the wall.

JIGSAW PUZZLE

It is great fun to make a homemade puzzle. You can control the complexity by using larger or smaller pieces and by varying the images you chose. Puzzles with small, all-over designs are more challenging to solve than landscapes, which usually have big sections of blue sky, distinctive clouds, fields, and foreground. In this puzzle we assembled a collage of faces of family and friends for an unusual image that's sure to please!

A

B

1. Prepare all the images you will be using for your puzzle. In your image-editing software, clean up and adjust the coloring of your scanned images, if necessary. Or open the images from your photo CD and, using the image-editing program, select the parts of the images you wish to use. Save these edited images to your hard drive. Make sure the resolutions and file types are all the same for consistency in sizing and in combining images. Also size each image to the approximate size you will want the picture to appear in your puzzle.

2. Decide on the dimensions of your puzzle: postcard-sized (6 x 4^1/$_4$ inches) or letter-sized (8^1/$_2$ x 11 inches), minus printer's margins.

3. Open a new document in your image-editing software, slightly larger than your target size. This will be your puzzle document. Open one of your face images and either completely knock out the background or leave a "halo" around the face. Copy this and paste it into your puzzle document. Continue opening your other images, cutting and pasting them into the master document, positioning the faces so they form an overall design. **(See Illustration A.)** For an easy puzzle, use fewer, larger faces and orient them all in one direction. To make it more challenging, use more faces, overlap them more tightly, and randomly rotate the images so that some faces are upside down, some are sideways, and others are at angles. Use other images as background, such as foliage or sky.

4. When you have completely covered the page, correct any minor imperfections and save the document.

5. Print this on your best paper and allow several hours for the ink to be absorbed into the paper.

6. In a well-ventilated area, spray the back of the paper with adhesive and adhere it to the cardboard. **(See Illustration B.)** When it's dry, trim the white margins with a craft knife and straightedge.

C

D

7. Using a pencil and scrap paper, plan your grid pattern, or design it in a drawing program. **(See Illustration C.)** For an easier puzzle, use fewer pieces and make them distinctly different. For advanced puzzle builders, make the pieces smaller and more similar in shape. Make sure to include the locking tabs so your puzzle will stay together.

8. Place a piece of carbon paper over your image and lay the grid pattern on top. With a pencil, trace the pattern onto your image.

9. Using a craft knife with a very sharp blade, cut along the puzzle piece edges. Reassemble the puzzle and test for fit. **(See Illustration D.)**

10. When finished, apply a protective coat of spray varnish, if desired. This will keep the pieces shiny and clean if they are to be used frequently. Allow to dry.

Creativity

• Mail this to someone as a real puzzler. Use it as an invitation to a party or a business meeting. Any image is potential for this technique, from wild designs concocted in your painting or drawing program to big or small pictures from your everyday life.

• A fun idea is to send one to a friend who hasn't written in a while. Design your layout to read, "I'm puzzled why you haven't written." When you have a complete project, put the separate pieces into a padded mailer and send it off. When the recipient assembles the pieces to read the message, you're sure to get a response!

PIN THE TAIL ON THE ZEBRA

Variations on the classic party game can be made at home. The huge image necessary for this project is achieved through a technique called tiling (see page 33). We have chosen a zebra to complement our safari birthday party, which began with the invitations shown on page 41. Nearly any animal can work for this, so the idea can easily be adapted to many kids' party themes.

What You'll Need

MATERIALS
High-quality paper, 8½ x 11 inches
Poster board or foam board, 24 x 30 inches

TOOLS
Light table (optional)
Scissors
Craft knife
Straightedge
Self-healing cutting mat
Low-tack tape
Spray adhesive
Double-sided tape
Removable mounting squares or plastic adhesive

ART
Scanned photograph or drawn image

SOFTWARE
Image-editing and drawing or painting programs

SKILL LEVEL
Advanced

COMPLETION TIME
3 hours

1. Find a fairly large and clear photo-graph of an animal, or create your own in a drawing or painting program. We found our zebra in a copyright-free collection of old illus-trations. (**See Illustration A.**) After scanning, we added color to the sky and grass. (**See Illustration B.**) If you are planning on using a bitmap file (black-and-white line art), save it in a format that your program will support (e.g., pict or tiff). If you are using a photo, scan and size it to match the dimensions of the finished product. (Ours measures 24 inches high by 30 inches wide.) Remember, if your original image was small, scaling it up will affect the image quality.

2. Remove the tail from the animal, and save it in a separate document to be printed in multiples later.

3. In your paint program, open a new document, sized to 15 x 12 inches. Make a large box of that dimen-sion, with a black stroke. Create a second box with a black stroke,

A

B

C

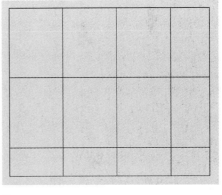

D

1 inch smaller in each dimension. Center this box on the first box. Between these two border edges, make random strokes with your brush tool using several closely related colors that suggest zebra striping. If your software allows you to work in layers, you can freely add strokes, cleaning up the edges of the border as a last step. **(See Illustration C.)** If not, you will need to open a new document. In this document, create an overall pattern of zebra stripes. Make guidelines that exactly indicate the width of your border. Select an area the size of one side of the border and copy and paste this into the main image. Position this, using the document edges as guidelines. Repeat this until the border is complete (top, bottom, and two sides). Open your colorized zebra image, and cut and paste it into this main image document, within the borders. Save your image in a format that you can open in your drawing program.

(continued on next page)

E

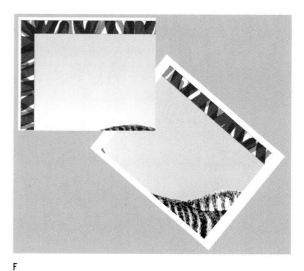

F

Tip

For such a large image, you may find it easier to work at 50 percent scale while image editing, then print the finished image at 200 percent. Remember to adjust your resolution accordingly: 72 ppi print resolution at full size; 144 ppi at half size.

4. In your drawing program, open a new document and adjust the page setup to reflect your desired finished dimensions. For our 24- x 30-inch measurement, that translates into three letter-sized pages down by four across, which allows plenty of space for printer margins. Place your composed image in the center of your page layout.

5. Before you print, select the tiling option that allows portions of the document to be printed on separate pages; consult your user's manual for specifics about this. **(See Illustration D** for a typical tiling grid.)

6. Print the document on your best paper. Allow the pieces to rest for at least an hour so the ink is fully absorbed.

7. Check that the panels register correctly, by using a light table or by holding the pieces up to a window. If there is some overlap **(see Illustration E)** tape them together in exact alignment using low-tack tape on the back of the paper. With a craft knife and straightedge, carefully cut along the edge of any overlapping pieces to trim away the excess below. Remove the tape. **(Illustration F** shows the same tiling layout but without the overlapped image area,

G

H

Creativity

• Change the game to reflect any topical theme. How about pin the wheel on the car, pin the tail on the rocket, or for a Halloween party, pin the hat on the witch or pin the grin on the jack o'lantern?

• Make an alphabet match-up. Create a large poster image with each letter of the alphabet, then give each child a cut-out letter to try to pin on the corresponding spot on the poster. Use lots of bright colors and make wild designs all over the background.

• If you want to play the game repeatedly, laminate the tail or other pin-on sections so they are more stable. You can buy page-sized sheets of self-laminating paper in stationery stores.

• Put each child's name on one of the tails and use them as place cards as well as game pieces!

so it would be trimmed right to the color edge.) Also trim off any white margins.

8. Using spray adhesive, adhere the upper right-hand corner piece to the poster board. Continue with the remaining pieces, butting seams and checking alignment as you go. **(See Illustration G.)** For long-term or heavy use, mount the image on foam board instead of poster board.

9. Place your isolated tail image on a page and add more tails if there is room. Print as many copies as you need. **(See Illustration H.)**

10. Cut out the tail pieces with scissors. Place a piece of double-sided tape at the base of each tail.

11. Use removable mounting squares or plastic adhesive to attach the board to the wall.

12. Remember the rules? One by one, blindfold the players, spin them around a few times, and let them loose to find the zebra. Have fun!

MEDALS

This great idea can be applied to fit a wide variety of occasions. We have made this one as a game prize for our African safari birthday party. Prepare a bunch of these to hand out as needed at the party. If you have a digital camera, you can take pictures on the spot, print them, trim them, and pop them into the medal frame for an instant success.

What You'll Need

MATERIALS
High-quality paper
Bristol board or firm cardboard
Jewelry pin back (available at
    craft stores) or safety pin
Grosgrain ribbon, about 4
    inches per medal
Card stock (optional)

TOOLS
Craft knife
Self-healing cutting mat
Circle cutter (optional)
Dimensional craft paint in
    appropriate colors
Acrylic polyurethane
Markers in appropriate colors
    (optional)
Double-sided tape (optional)

ART
Drawn images, clip art,
    decorative fonts

SOFTWARE
Painting and drawing programs

SKILL LEVEL
Intermediate

COMPLETION TIME
2½ hours, plus drying time

1. On paper, sketch your ideas for each medal. Organize whatever text you will need and decide whether you want to use a photograph or a fake coin as the central piece. To make a medal without photo inserts, simply leave out those steps and use words or small clip art images.

2. In a drawing program, draw a 3-inch-diameter circle. Using a text tool, type your information and style the text so that it forms a complete circle with a 2-inch diameter inner space left blank. By using gradients, you can make the medallion and the text resemble engraved gold, silver, or bronze. Have fun creating the metal textures. We have a different color background to signify different awards. **(See Illustration A.)**

3. Copy and paste several more of these medallions to make the best use of your paper.

4. Draw a rectangle 3 inches long by ³/₄ inches high. This will be the bar at the top of the medallion. Add a bright color or a strong pattern, such as vertical or diagonal bars. We made zebra stripes to complement our theme. Copy and paste these in blank spaces on your layout, allowing the same number of bars as you have circles.

5. On your best paper, print as many copies as you need plus a few extras. Allow to dry for about an hour.

A

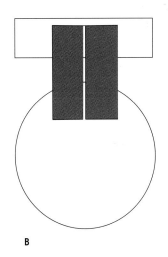

B

6. Cut out the circles and bars, leaving about $1/8$ inch of white space all around, which will be trimmed later. Glue these to the Bristol board or cardboard. Allow to dry.

7. Trim the shapes to their exact size. To achieve a smooth circle, use a circle cutter, or find a small round object to use as a cutting guide and trim around it with a craft knife.

8. Using a color-coordinated shade, outline each bar and circle with a thin line of dimensional paint. Embellish the pieces with additional paint as desired. If you will be adding photographs, place a second circle of dimensional paint about $1/2$ inch in from the inside circle, around the central image. Allow the paint to dry thoroughly, overnight or per manufacturer's instructions.

9. Pour a small amount of polyurethane into the little areas created by the dimensional paint. Do not overfill. Do this on a flat surface in a well-ventilated area where you can leave the project for several hours without disturbing the pieces, since the polyurethane takes time to dry.

10. When the pieces have completely dried, clean up any imperfections. If you used Bristol board with a white core, color the rim with a marker.

11. Cut a 4-inch length of ribbon in half. Glue one end of each half to the back of the medallion and the other end to the bar. **(See Illustration B.)**

12. Glue a pin back to the back of the bar and allow to dry. For a quick approach, use a piece of double-sided tape, which is not as permanent but easy to do for small kids.

13. To add a photograph, select the image in an image-editing program, crop it in a 2-inch-wide circle, and print this on heavy card stock. Trim it in a circle and attach it to the front of the medallion with double-sided tape. Now pin it on the winner and watch for a glow of pride!

Creativity

• You can make military-style medals, or fun, everyone-is-a-winner medals. The ribbon is integral to the look of your finished reward, so choose patterned grosgrain or pretty satin for a more lush look. Beautiful velvet ribbons would add distinction, too.

• If cutting out circles seems tough, try squares turned on edge to make diamonds, or triangles.

fabric projects

Transferring images onto fabric opens up a world of possibilities. The process can be accomplished by either of two methods: by using transfer paper, from which the image is then ironed onto fabric, or by printing the image directly onto fabric that has been prepared to load into your printer. The first two projects in this chapter, the napkins and T-shirt, utilize transfer paper. The other three incorporate variations on the direct-printing technique. The sachets are printed on nonfusible interfacing, available in fabric stores. The images for the quilt are printed on Canon fabric sheets, sold in office supply stores. And the jacket project explains how to make your own fabric sheets on which to print images.

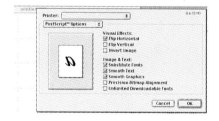

Before printing an image that will be transferred, be sure to reverse anything that would look wrong flopped.

Transfer Paper

Transfer paper is a specially prepared media that readily accepts color ink and allows you to heat-transfer your printed image to any suitable surface, including many types of fabric. A variety of brands can be found at computer stores, stationery stores, office supply stores, and some warehouse-type retailers. Some types of transfer paper can also be purchased from computer catalogs or directly through the manufacturer. Check printer manufacturers' Web sites for more information. Some of the most popular brands are Hewlett-Packard T-shirt Transfers, Epson Iron-on Transfer Paper, and Canon T-shirt Transfers.

Before you print, review the instructions for both your printer and the transfer paper you bought; there may be special settings to optimize your results. You may also want to make some sample transfers on similar fabrics to gain some practice at this technique before trying it on your actual project.

The transfer method automatically creates a mirror image of your design, since you have to place the printed transfer paper face down to apply it to the fabric. Many designs will be unaffected by this, since they will look fine when reversed. But if your design contains any text or if your image would look wrong flopped, remember to reverse any such images before printing. All image-editing software can accomplish this. Some printers and scanners are even equipped to handle this automatically, so check your owner's manual for more information.

Once your image is printed and has dried, trim the transfer paper nearly flush to the images, but leave a small tab on each piece so that you can easily pull off the paper backing after the image has been transferred. Since most types of transfer paper require that the backing paper be removed immediately after pressing and the transfer will therefore be very hot, this little tab makes it much easier to avoid burnt fingers. Check the instructions that came with your transfer paper for specifics about removing the backing paper.

Ironing

The actual transfer process requires the heat of an iron and a firm, heat-resistant surface. You can use an ironing board, but you may not get the best results working directly on the ironing board's padded surface. Try adding a firm, heat-safe layer such as plywood or stiff cardboard beneath the area receiving the transfer. When working with an item such as a T-shirt, place this layer inside the shirt rather than under the whole garment so that there is only one layer of fabric between the iron and the firm surface. Other firm, heat-resistant surfaces such as a table may be used instead of an ironing board, especially when pressing large areas that may not fit comfortably on the ironing board.

When ironing the transfer, don't slide the iron back and forth; this will distort the image. Begin by gently applying pressure with the iron in one spot for a short time to anchor the image, then lift the iron, reposition it, and press until the entire image area has been transferred. Consult the transfer paper manufacturer's instructions for specifics on ironing time. Remember that a small image heats up very quickly since the iron will cover the whole picture at once; larger images take a bit longer because you have to reposition the iron each time you want to fuse a new area of the image. When you think the image is fully fused to the fabric, use the small tab to lift a tiny bit of the backing paper and check to be sure the entire image has been completely transferred. As soon as it has, remove the backing paper.

Interfacing

Various brands of interfacing are sold at fabric stores; Pellon™ is perhaps the most widely known. Be sure to purchase the nonfusible type, which is generally sold in 24-inch widths. When you cut the interfacing into $8^{1}/_{2}$- x 11-inch sheets, it can be loaded into your paper tray and be printed on directly. You may want to test different thicknesses to see which types will work best in your printer, and to observe how the color saturation changes as the inks hit the material.

Printing on Fabric

One manufacturer, Canon, makes pre-prepared muslin sheets that load easily and conveniently into your printer. They come in 9- x 14-inch sheets. Some printers may not accommodate this width, so you may have to trim the media; check your owner's manual. Also be aware that some older-model printers may require the inks to be chemically set. Read the instructions carefully and test a small piece first.

With inexpensive muslin and some plastic-coated freezer paper, you can easily create your own fabric sheets to load into the printer. See the jacket project (pages 107–11) for directions.

When you print an image on white fabric, the images will retain exactly the same colors as your original photos. If you want to try printing on fabric other than white, take your photographs or printed images to the fabric store and look at some combinations. Have fun selecting the fabrics. There are no hard and fast rules, so check out out florals, dots, stripes, and plaids. Just remember that it will be harder to keep your seams looking professional if you use stripes or plaids (you can drive yourself nuts trying to match plaids). Mixing and matching patterns is fun, so experiment with some unexpected combinations.

To ease removal of the transfer backing paper, remember to leave a little tab when trimming around an image.

CLOTH NAPKINS

This great hostess gift takes practically no time to make. Buy beautiful linen or cotton napkins by the dozen, then personalize by transferring images onto them. Bundle several of the napkins together for a beautiful presentation.

First, plan your theme, then look for an image or a photograph that best illustrates your idea. You'll need an image that is in one complete piece and can be isolated from its background. A fern frond, a butterfly, a face, or a building all work well. Use a digital camera to capture a garden flower, or look on the CD-ROMS that come with software programs for appropriate clip art. Remember to reverse the items if necessary, since the transfer process creates a mirror image.

What You'll Need

MATERIALS
T-shirt transfer paper
White cocktail napkins

TOOLS
Scissors
Iron and ironing board

ART
Scanned photographs, clip art

SOFTWARE
Image-editing and drawing
  programs

SKILL LEVEL
Easy

COMPLETION TIME
1 hour

A

1. Select your central image or images, choosing appropriately so that the outer edges of the napkin will form a natural flow around the item. We found some beautiful Victorian fruit and flower drawings. **(See Illustration A.)** If you want to add text, remember to reverse it.

2. Arrange the images so they will fit on one sheet of transfer paper, with some white space surrounding each one.

3. Print the images on the transfer paper. Remember to review the loading instructions for your particular machine.

4. Trim the transfer paper nearly flush to the images, but leave a small tab on each piece so that you can easily pull off the paper backing after the image has been transferred. (It will be very hot, so the tab makes it much easier to avoid burnt fingers!)

5. Remove any water from the iron and set the temperature gauge to the hottest setting. Preheat your iron for about ten minutes.

6. Arrange the napkin on your ironing surface. Iron the spot where you will be placing the image. **(See Illustration B for placement of the art.)**

7. Place the transfer paper on the napkin surface, image side down. Press the image onto the napkin, following manufacturer's directions about length of ironing time. Lift and reposition the iron to reach a new area of the transfer; don't drag the iron over the paper or you'll risk moving the transfer and smearing the image. Remember to avoid ironing over the small tab you left for removal of the backing paper. (See page 94 for more about ironing transfers.)

8. When the image is completely fused into the fabric and while it is still very warm, pull the corner tab, testing when you start. If it comes up easily, remove the backing paper; if not, reheat the area. If you are using the newer transfers that can be peeled when cool, follow the manufacturer's directions.

9. Transfer the remaining images onto the napkins. They are ready to use after cooling to room temperature. Package them beautifully for gift giving, or enjoy them yourself. Follow manufacturer's instructions on washing. We've found that washing in cool water on a gentle cycle seems to work best.

Creativity

• At holidays, transfer clip art images that reinforce the celebratory mood.

• For a housewarming party, drive by the new place a day or two before the event and take a digital photo of the new home. Use this image on your napkins for a nice sentimental touch.

• For weddings and christenings, include some text that commemorates the big event. These precious keepsakes will be passed down from one generation to the next.

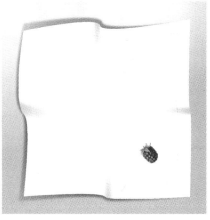

B

EMBELLISHED T-SHIRT

What You'll Need

MATERIALS
White cotton or polyester-
   cotton T-shirt
T-shirt transfer paper, 2 sheets
   per shirt

TOOLS
Scissors or craft knife
Self-healing cutting mat
Iron and ironing board

ART
Scanned photographs, clip art

SOFTWARE
Drawing or painting program

SKILL LEVEL
Intermediate

COMPLETION TIME
2 hours

Of course you can imagine making a T-shirt with iron-on transfers, but let's go one step further to make this T-shirt a little out of the ordinary. The key is to consider the entire shirt as a potential surface, to "think outside the box" when envisioning your finished creation. Break up the space into pieces and place parts of your image in unexpected areas. Add images to the sleeves and to the back for a more integrated design.

Plan the theme of the shirt first, then look for images and photographs to support your idea. Try taking pictures of your garden to use for an overall floral design. Or leaf through your family photo album (real or digital) for further inspiration.

You will need one large image for the front of the shirt, a smaller image (about half the size of the main image) for the back of the shirt near the neckline, and a small image (about one-fourth the size of the main image) that will be repeated on each sleeve. Our project is sized for an adult's medium shirt; adjust the image sizes as needed for your project.

1. Scan your chosen photographs or use digital images from your own collection or from clip art libraries. Remember to reverse any items as necessary, since the transfer process creates a mirror image. Enhance the design of your central image so the outer edges form a natural flow around the central motif. To accomplish this in your image-editing software, start with one image, select a second image, and place it on top of the original. Move it into position, then add additional images until you form a pleasing overall composition. The large picture should be about 7 x 9 inches. For the other images, select either a reduced version of your main motif or elements from it, each appropriately sized. Your sleeve images should each be about 2$\frac{1}{2}$ x 2$\frac{1}{2}$ inches. **(See Illustration A,** which shows our chosen back neckline images at the top, sleeve image at the upper right, and central front image below.)

A

B

C

2. Arrange the smaller images on one page so they will fit on one sheet of transfer paper, with some white space between the images to allow for cutting area. Place the larger front image on another page, to be printed on a separate sheet of transfer paper. **(See Illustrations B and C.)**

3. Print the images on the T-shirt transfer paper. Remember to review the loading instructions for your machine so that you print on the specially prepared surface.

4. Trim the transfer paper nearly flush to the images, but leave a small tab sticking out from each piece so that you can pull off the paper backing after it has been transferred.

5. Remove any water from the iron, set the temperature gauge to the hottest setting, and preheat your iron for about ten minutes. Arrange the T-shirt on your ironing surface. To ensure a firm pressing surface if you're working on a padded ironing board, place a scrap of plywood or heavy cardboard inside the shirt underneath the area receiving the transfer. Press the fabric smooth in the area where you will be placing the image.

6. Place the transfer paper on the shirt surface, image side down. Locate the small tab you will use to pull off the backing paper with and be careful not to iron this tab down. First, carefully anchor the transfer paper to the fabric with brief all-over pressure, then iron in sections. Be sure to lift, reposition, and press. Do not slide the iron—this will distort the image. Follow manufacturer's directions for length of ironing time.

7. When the image is completely fused to the fabric and still very warm (be careful not to burn yourself), pull the removal tab and peel off the backing paper. If you are using the newer transfers that can be peeled when cool, follow manufacturer's directions.

8. Complete the transfer of all the images onto your shirt. Once the shirt cools to room temperature it is ready to wear. Follow manufacturer's directions on washing. We have found that turning the shirt inside out and washing with cool water on a gentle cycle seems to work best.

Creativity

• Think about placing a person's name in big letters all around the bottom of the shirt. Each letter might be made up of an image or textures created on your computer. Or place the images so that they form a band around the sleeves, across the chest, and over the back. Another idea is to place soft floral images completely around the neckline for a delicate and feminine look.

SACHET

Although there is a little bit of sewing involved, this is actually a very easy project and you can complete a beautiful sachet in about two hours. The computer gives you the flexibility to personalize your images and the actual construction of the sachet takes only a short time. We made two designs for our sachet—one for the front and one for the back—using text as well as patterns for our designs. You'll be printing your image directly on nonfusible interfacing (see page 95 for more information on interfacing). These sachets aren't meant to be washed or cleaned, so there is no need for any additional treatment once they are printed; just make them and enjoy!

What You'll Need

MATERIALS
Medium-weight nonfusible
  interfacing, ½ yard (enough
  for 2 sachets)
Potpourri, about ¼ cup per
  sachet
¼- or ⅛-inch-wide double-faced
  satin ribbon, about 1 yard per
  sachet

TOOLS
Iron and ironing board
Scissors
Sewing machine or needle and
  thread
Funnel (optional)
Decorative-edge scissors or
  pinking shears (optional)
Glue gun (optional)

ART
Clip art or scanned images of
  flowers, fabrics, patterns, and
  typeface elements

SOFTWARE
Image-editing and drawing
  programs

SKILL LEVEL
Intermediate

COMPLETION TIME
2 hours

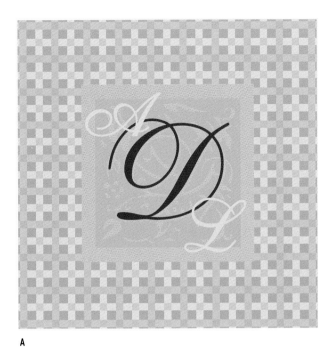

A

1. Using a drawing program, create a box 7 x 7 inches. The color of the box stroke can be any tone, since this will be trimmed off in a later step. Fill the box with a scanned image of a pattern or use one of the patterned fills available in your drawing program.

2. Draw a box 3 x 3 inches, center it within the first box, and fill it with a coordinating color.

3. Embellish the inner box with a monogram, a name, or a brief message. This is a great project to use "dingbats" or other decorative elements. Using a bold typeface, type the desired text and size it to fit. We used initials on one **(see Illustration A)** and repeated a name on each side of the other **(see Illustration B)**. Adjust the color to coordinate with your ribbon and your decorative images.

4. If you want a different design for the other side of the sachet, create

it the same way you set up the first one.

5. Cut the interfacing into 8¹/₂- x 11-inch sheets. Make sure the sheets are perfectly smooth. If necessary, press with a medium-hot iron.

6. Load one sheet of interfacing into the paper tray just as you would a sheet of paper. If your printer has a thickness lever, move it to maximum so that the print heads do not hit the fabric as they travel back and forth. If your printer doesn't have a thickness lever, test it out on the interfacing before printing your project. Print your image, using settings most appropriate for your equipment. When the image is finished printing, let it rest for at least half an hour to ensure the inks are fully absorbed.

7. Cut the 7-inch square along the outside lines. You are going to trim this edge again later, so complete accuracy is not essential here.

(continued on next page)

Creativity

• Personalization is a nice touch: think about adding an inspirational quote around the outer edge. Or use a scanned image of fabric—a plaid or a paisley design would look great.

• Coordinate the scent of the potpourri with a photographic image of a flower. In the next two projects you will learn how to print on fabric sheets that you purchase or create—try printing the sachets on silk for a luxurious touch.

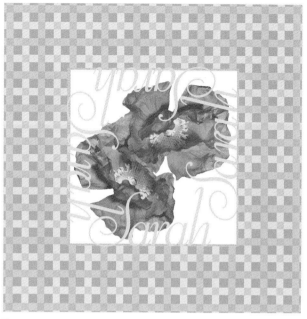

B

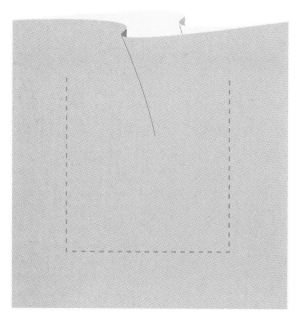

C

8. Print the other side of the sachet on another sheet of interfacing. Once it's dry, trim along the outside lines.

9. Align the two pieces wrong sides together and sew them (by hand or machine) along the edge of the inner box on three sides. Leave the top open to allow for the insertion of the potpourri. **(See Illustration C.)**

10. Using a funnel or rolled-up paper, pour the potpourri into the opening. Do not overfill—it should be only about one-third to half full.

11. Sew up the fourth side, completely enclosing the potpourri material. For a bit of added decoration, trim the outside edges with decorative-edge scissors or pinking shears.

12. Tie a piece of narrow ribbon into a bow and sew or glue it to the sachet. We also chose to frame the design with more of the ribbon, securing it with a glue gun.

MEMORY QUILT

Create a beautiful quilt that features photographs from your most precious memories—family get-togethers, college, trips, or other events. Our quilt was inspired by vacations but the field is wide open. We scanned each individual picture from a group of photographs, then adjusted the colors and cropped the images so that they made a pleasing overall composition. Imagine the surprise a family member will have when presented with a quilt whose colors, images, and every detail reflect cherished events. This is a wonderful way to make new memories and family traditions.

We selected traditional quilt fabrics—calico cottons and other small, overall patterned fabrics—but you can use any fabrics that you are comfortable working with. (See the general fabric guidelines on pages 94–95 for more information.) Before you print, review the instructions for both your printer and the fabric sheets, since there may be special settings to optimize your results. Make a test sample if this is the first time you have used this technique.

Note that the fabric measurements are given for the standard 45-inch fabric width, and remember that the Canon fabric sheets are sold in 9- x 14-inch pieces.

What You'll Need

MATERIALS
10 Canon fabric sheets
Fabric A, ½ yard
Fabric B, ¼ yard
Fabric C, ⅝ yard
Fabric D, 2 yards
Batting

TOOLS
Scissors
Rotary cutter
Ruler
Self-healing cutting mat
Sewing machine
Coordinating thread
Pins or basting thread and
    needle
Iron and ironing board

ART
Computerized photographs,
    clip art

SOFTWARE
Image-editing program;
    drawing program

SKILL LEVEL
Advanced

COMPLETION TIME
12 hours

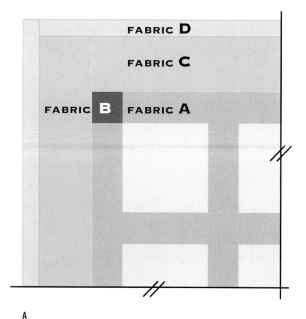

FABRIC **D**

FABRIC **C**

FABRIC **B** FABRIC **A**

A

B

1. Select the event you wish to commemorate and gather your images, either with a digital camera or by scanning photos. Supplement them with clip art images if you wish. Study your choices to arrive at a color scheme that will tie the selected images together and coordinate with the fabric you select for a pleasing overall effect. (We chose nine photos as the main images and four small images as design motifs.) The large pictures should measure 7 x 7 inches, the smaller ones 2$^1/_2$ x 2$^1/_2$ inches. Gang up the smaller images to maximize your fabric sheet layout; all four images should fit on one sheet, with $^1/_4$ inch seam allowance around all photos.

2. Print the images on the fabric sheets, following manufacturer's instructions. Trim each image with a $^1/_4$-inch margin on all four sides.

3. Cut the fabrics and batting as indicated below. Note that $^1/_4$-inch seam allowances are included in these measurements. **(See Illustration A.)**

   Fabric A, inner sashing: 12 pieces, each 3 x 7$^1/_2$ inches
   Fabric A, outer sashing: 4 pieces, each 3 x 26$^1/_2$ inches
   Fabric B, small corner squares: 4 pieces, each 3 x 3 inches
   Fabric B, channel: 1 strip, 3 x 41 inches (this will be stitched along the top edge of the back in case you want to hang the quilt)
   Fabric C, top and bottom borders: 2 strips, each 5$^1/_2$ x 31$^1/_2$ inches
   Fabric C, side borders: 2 strips, each 5$^1/_2$ x 41$^1/_2$ inches
   Fabric D, backing: 1 piece, 41$^1/_2$ x 41$^1/_2$ inches
   Fabric D, binding: 2 strips, each 3$^1/_2$ x 41$^1/_2$ inches; 2 strips, each 3$^1/_2$ x 42 inches
   Battting: 1 piece, 41$^1/_2$ inches by 41$^1/_2$ inches

4. The quilt front will be pieced in rows. Remember that all seam allowances are $^1/_4$ inch. For the first row, sew the first 7-inch photo square image to a strip of fabric A. Sew the second photo square to

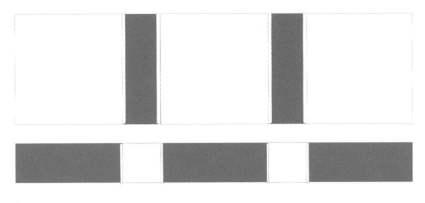

C

the other edge of the strip, then sew another strip of fabric A to the other edge of the second photo square, followed by the third photo square. **(See Illustration B.)** Press seams toward the strip fabric, away from the image. **(See Illustration C**, top diagram.)

5. Construct the second row using a strip of fabric A, followed by one of the small photo squares, then another strip of fabric A, a second small photo square, and finally a third strip of fabric A. Press seams toward the strip fabric, away from the image. **(See Illustration C**, lower diagram.) Repeat steps 4 and 5 to complete the other three rows.

6. Sew each of these rows together in order, pinning carefully to align all the seams.

7. For the outside sashing with the small squares at each corner, begin by sewing one of the long strips of fabric A to the left side of the main quilt front, then sew another long strip to the right side. **(See Illustration D.)** Press all seams toward the fabric strip, away from the image squares.

8. Sew one of the fabric B squares to each end of the two remaining fabric A strips. Press seams away from the image square. Pinning carefully to align seams, sew one of these pieced rows along the top of the main quilt section and one along the bottom. You now have your main patchwork and image area.

9. Next comes the solid border. Start by sewing one of the longer fabric C strips to the left side of the main quilt front, then sew the other longer strip to the right hand side. Press all seams toward the border fabric, away from the main area. Attach one of the shorter fabric C strips to the top of the quilt and the other to the bottom.

10. Now you will attach the quilt backing and the batting to the pieced surface. On a large, flat surface, lay out your backing square, wrong side up. Spread your batting over this, smoothing and adjusting as necessary. On top of the batting, lay your quilt front, right side up. Pin or baste these layers together carefully at regular intervals to allow ease of handling and quilting.

11. Using coordinating thread in your sewing machine, stitch in the "ditch" formed by the seams.

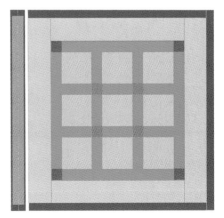

D

E

(continued on next page)

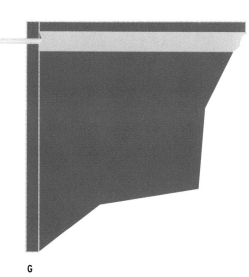

G

F

Creativity

• Gather family tree materials and arrange the successive rows in the quilt with photos and images from each generation. If the older images are all in black and white or sepia, use your image-editing software to adjust the tones of the color images to blend well for a coordinated look.

• If someone you know has just had a baby, suggest to friends that they all send images (in a common format, such as JPEG files) via e-mail to create a very modern group quilt.

Continue to sew along each seam line until all selected seams have been stitched. Add decorative quilting stitches in the border areas, if desired.

12. Trim any excess batting material and trim up all four sides so that the shape is square and even. Remove any pins or basting stitches.

13. Prepare the two slightly shorter strips of fabric D by ironing a $^{1}/_{4}$ inch fold along one long edge. Position the first strip so that the seam falls $1^{1}/_{2}$ inches from the outside edge of the quilt. **(See Illustration E.)** At this point, you can use whatever method is most comfortable for you to attach the binding—either by sewing the front and back edges in one operation or by sewing the binding onto the front edge, then folding it over and catch-stitching it by hand on the reverse side. **(See Illustration F.)** Sew the second strip to the opposite side in the same manner. Sew the two longer strips to the two side edges so that they cover the first strips at the corners. Tuck the edges in, and stitch over the ends to finish off the binding.

14. Using a whipstitch, sew the remaining strip of fabric B along the top of the back of the quilt, forming a channel into which you can insert a dowel that will allow you to hang the quilt. **(See Illustration G.)**

15. This is an heirloom, so make sure to sew a label on the back indicating the dates involved, the maker of the quilt, and the event it commemorates.

GRAPHICS JACKET

This is a fairly complex project that requires some advanced planning. The instructions are general, since you will need to adapt this to your purchased pattern, personal taste, size, fabric selections, and other choices. Simple patterns with few pieces work best for this project. Read through the instructions, figure out what you want to accomplish, and use our directions as general project guidelines, adapting as necessary. Note that the fabric measurements are given for the standard 45-inch fabric width. Choose fabrics that coordinate well with the images you select to adorn your jacket.

If you absolutely must have a washable jacket, use washable notions and prewash all the pieces; the printed fabric pieces should be washed both before and after printing. Even with all-washable materials, however, the images will eventually fade, so it's best to consider this jacket a "dry-clean only" garment. But the effort will be well worth it: since this creation ventures into the "wearable art" category, be prepared for a very satisfying result that will win rave reviews from family, friends, and even people you run into on the street.

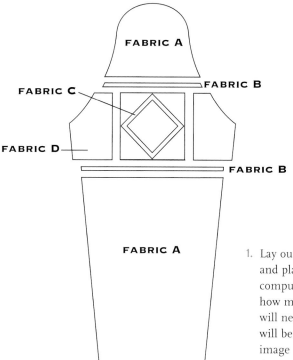

FABRIC A

FABRIC C

FABRIC B

FABRIC D

FABRIC B

FABRIC A

A

1. Lay out the jacket pattern pieces and plan where you will place the computer-printed pieces. Decide how many printed images you will need and how big the images will be. Calculate how high your image panels will be. Divide the three main pattern pieces (front, back, and sleeve) into three sections: top section, to be cut from fabric A; center section, comprising the pieced assemblage of the printed-image fabric along with fabrics B, C, and D; and bottom section, which will also be cut from fabric A. **(See Illustration A.)** Remember to add seam allowances. Calculate the layout and yardage for the contrasting fabrics. Because this jacket requires some "as-you-go" adjustments, be sure to have some extra fabric for design changes.

2. Choose a theme for your images. (We used nineteenth-century poster graphics.) Open your image in a painting or image-editing program and size it to 5 x 5 inches. Adjust the color and clean up the image. Crop the picture in a diamond shape, consistent with the size required for your jacket. Repeat this with each of your images, saving each as a separate file. (We used seven images: two front, three back, one per sleeve.)

3. Cut 10- x 13-inch pieces of muslin, one for each image. Wet them under running water. Pour $1/4$ cup fabric softener and $1/4$ cup water into a sealable plastic bag. Put the muslin in the bag, seal it, and squish the fabric around in the solution. Let them soak about 15 minutes.

4. Rinse the muslin under running water, let the excess water drain, and iron the pieces flat.

5. Cut pieces of freezer paper $9^1/_2$ x $12^1/_2$ inches, one for each image. Place a piece of muslin on your ironing board and position the freezer paper on top, shiny side down. With the iron on a medium setting and no steam, iron one piece of freezer paper on each piece of muslin.

6. Trim the fabrics to $8^1/_2$ x 11 inches using a ruler and a very sharp rotary cutter or craft knife.

7. Spray the fabric pieces heavily with anti-static spray and allow to dry completely before printing.

8. When dry, feed the sheets into your printer just as you would a sheet of paper. Print your images on the fabric sheets and allow to dry for half an hour.

9. Spray the images with artist's fixative, using a light touch so they don't become stiff.

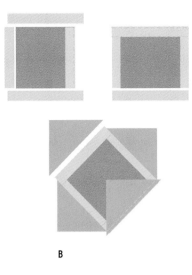

B

10. Cut out main jacket pieces (front, back, and sleeves) from fabric A, following pattern instructions.

11. Cut two strips from fabric B, which will form the upper and lower borders of the design panel for the jacket back; four strips for the front; and four additional strips for the sleeves. Our strips were 1 inch wide. Here is how to calculate the length of the strips for each pattern piece. Lay out the front pattern piece and measure across the widest horizontal point, the area across the chest to the underarm section. Repeat this for the back pattern piece, measuring at exactly the same point. Then measure the sleeve pattern across the widest horizontal point, from armpit to armpit. This will ensure that you will have a continuous band of inserted fabrics traveling across the front, over the sleeves, around the back, and so on. Our front pieces were approximately 20 inches each; the back piece was about 40 inches; and each sleeve was about 18 inches. Double-check all your measurements before cutting.

12. Cut strips of fabric C to attach to the four sides of each image. **(See Illustration B.)** To surround each of our 5-inch-square images with 1-inch wide borders we needed to cut two strips measuring $5^1/_2$ x $1^1/_2$ inches (including $1/_4$ inch seam allowance) and two strips measuring $7^1/_2$ x $1^1/_2$ inches. Since we used seven images, we cut a total of fourteen strips measuring $5^1/_2$ x $1^1/_2$ inches, and fourteen strips measuring $7^1/_2$ x $1^1/_2$ inches.

13. Cut your computer-printed fabric to the final dimensions, leaving a $1/_4$-inch seam allowance around each central image. Since our finished images needed to be 5 x 5 inches, the cutting dimensions were $5^1/_2$ x $5^1/_2$ inches.

14. Cut 28 triangles from fabric D, sizing them to form a complete square when sewn around the diamond-shaped image pieces. **(See Illustration B.)** The length of the longest side of your triangle will equal the length of the longer border strip you cut in step 12, including seam allowance. Since our longer border strip was $7^1/_2$ inches long, our triangle's longest side was $7^1/_2$ inches.

(continued on next page)

Creativity

• The possibilities are endless using this technique. Create heirloom pieces by incorporating family photos. Show up at the next reunion with images from the past highlighted in your apparel. Create a special wedding, birthday, or anniversary treat for a loved one.

• Needless to say, the diamond design does not have to be followed. Straight lines are easier, but any form of piecing can be accommodated. This particular design resembles Seminole piecing, a quilter's technique based on designs made by the Seminole Indians in the early part of the nineteenth century, whereby small pieces of new fabrics in solid, bright colors were sewn together in intricate patterns. Browse through some quilting sources for more ideas to adapt.

• Many sewing and craft magazines (*Threads,* for instance) offer patterns for garments that would suit this technique because they are designed with a minimum of seams and curved cutting lines.

C

15. Once you've pieced these squares, cut ten pieces of fabric C to fill in the side areas. To calculate the size of these filler pieces, measure the height of the computer-printed fabric piece, including the fabric C border and seam allowances. (Remember, the pieced squares are being rotated 90 degrees in the assembly step, so the height from top to bottom point is longer than the length of one side.) Subtract this number from the length of the bands you cut in step 11, then divide this number in half. For example, our finished pieced section is $8^1/_2$ inches square. So we subtracted 9 ($8^1/_2$ inches plus $^1/_2$ inch seam allowance) from 18 (the width of the sleeve band created in step 11) to get 9 inches, which was divided by 2, giving us the dimensions for each of the two side pieces: $4^1/_2$ x 9 inches. You will need two side pieces for the back section, two each for the front pieces and two each for the sleeves, for a total of ten filler pieces. **(See Illustration C.)**

16. Begin piecing the front of the jacket by sewing one of the shorter ($5^1/_2$-inch) strips of fabric C to a side of one of the images. Sew a second short strip to the opposite side. Press seams toward fabric C. Attach two of the longer strips to the remaining two sides and press the seams toward fabric C. Complete this process for each of the seven images.

17. Now sew a triangle of fabric D to one edge of a printed and pieced diamond. Continue to sew the triangles and diamonds together until you have a complete square. Repeat this process for all the printed diamonds until you have seven completed squares. Sew three squares together for the back, and then sew two sets of two together for the front pieces. The remaining squares will be used for each of the sleeves. Press all seams away from the images. Sew one of the side pieces of Fabric D to each end of these assembled strips. Also add a side piece to each of the remaining squares that will form the sleeve sections.

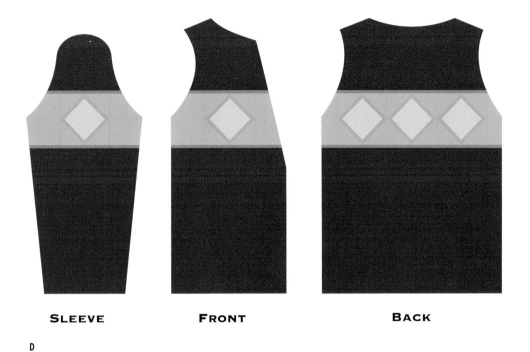

SLEEVE **FRONT** **BACK**

D

18. Sew fabric B strips across the top and bottom of each of these panels. Press seams toward fabric B.

19. For the back pattern piece, center the pieced panel against the top section of fabric A and align it carefully. Sew this assembled strip, right sides together, to the fabric A section. Align the bottom piece of fabric A, right sides together, and sew this in place. Trim this entire

section neatly to match the outline of the pattern piece. Repeat this process for the jacket front pieces and the sleeves. **(See Illustration D.)** Press all seams.

20. Once all the individual portions of the jacket are assembled, complete the jacket construction following the pattern directions, including lining, if called for.

CHAPTER SIX

decorating your home

PICTURE FRAME

What You'll Need

MATERIALS
High-quality paper
Bristol board
Matte acrylic or gouache paint
  in coordinating color
Photograph to be framed
Thin acetate sheet (optional)

TOOLS
Craft knife
Ruler
Paintbrush
Spray mount adhesive or glue
  stick
Glue gun and glue sticks, white
  glue, or double-sided tape

ART
Texture clip art, scanned-in
  marbled paper, or altered
  image; decorative font

SOFTWARE
Painting and page-layout
  programs

SKILL LEVEL
Intermediate

COMPLETION TIME
2½ hours

Rather than simply giving someone a framed photo, enhanced it by personalizing the frame to suit the contents. Think of those beautiful Italian hand-marbled papers sold in expensive, fabulous stationery stores—you can easily replicate that look with your computer to create a lovely frame that makes a very special gift.

First, select your photograph. If you choose one that has been processed by the traditional photo-emulsion method, have it professionally printed in the correct size; here we use a photo with an image area of 4 x 6 inches. Notice what colors are dominant and what tones are most appropriate for the theme you want to convey. Our project features a bright shot of twins, so we had plenty of colors to choose from. We decided to pick up the colors from the denim so that our frame would complement the colorful photo.

You can select a pattern from your image library of clip art sources, perhaps basing it on marbled paper as we did. If you cannot locate a marbled pattern on the computer, you can probably find suitable paper at an art supply store, then scan it to a file on your hard drive using a flatbed color scanner. Test the resolution settings to get the optimum trade-off between dpi and storage considerations. You can make great patterns using the filter features of your image-editing software. Experiment with some of those features—you'll be gratified by what you can accomplish.

December 13, 1999

MEG ❀ ⚘ CHASE

A

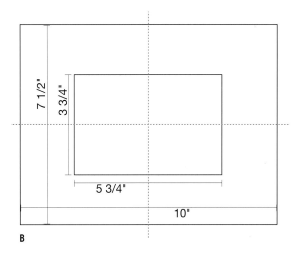

7 1/2"

3 3/4"

5 3/4"

10"

B

1. Create your overall design, either by opening a scanned image, using clip art, or by creating it from scratch in your image-editing software. We took colored lines and used filters to swirl the color around. Then we tiled the resulting image to arrive at four pieces that came together to create the overall image. In your painting program, size the image to the largest print area allowed by your printer.

2. Print two copies on your best paper; these will be used to cover the back of the frame.

3. Return to the original image and, using your "Save as" command, rename and save it. This will be the front of your frame. Type your message, placing it $1^1/4$ inches from the bottom edge and centering between the left and right edges. The letters should be fairly large (about 60-point type, depending on the font you choose) but keep the text line under 6 inches long. You may also want to run some text across the top of the frame, about $1^1/4$ inches from the top edge. (We placed the photo's date in this space.) **(See**

Illustration A.) Enhance the text by using bright colors or drop shadows. You can also change the opacity of the type to achieve interesting effects. Adjusting opacity will create a translucency that allows the marbled paper texture to show through the text.

4. Print your marbled design on your best paper. Do not use card stock or heavier-weight papers because they do not crease and fold cleanly.

5. Using a craft knife and ruler, cut four pieces of Bristol board: three pieces each $7^1/2$ x 10 inches and one piece 3 x 6 inches (for the easel stand). Make sure your printed pattern will cover the frame; if not, trim your boards down to fit. Cut out an area $5^3/4$ x $3^3/4$ inches at the exact center of two $7^1/2$- x 10-inch Bristol board pieces. **(See Illustration B.)** Glue these two pieces of Bristol board together and let dry. (We find it easier to locate, cut, and handle thinner board and then glue two layers together than to work with thicker board. If you have access to the materials and tools, you can use a board $1/8$ to $1/4$ inch thick.)

(continued on next page)

Tips

• If this is a commercial project, make sure that the pattern is copyright free or that you obtain the artist's permission to use the work.

• If you want to accommodate a layer of glass or acrylic, it's easy to do so with an extra layer of cardboard that is the same thickness as your glass or acrylic sheet, typically ⅜ inch. Here is how to calculate it: if your photo image area is to be 4 by 6 inches, then make this extra layer the same overall dimensions of your frame with a 4¼- x 6¼-inch window inside. Glue the front frame section to this additional piece and then cover the frame with your marbled paper. Proceed as above, but before gluing the back to the front, insert the glass or acrylic, cut to size, in this holder. Be careful if you use glass because if it breaks, the frame cannot be opened without damage.

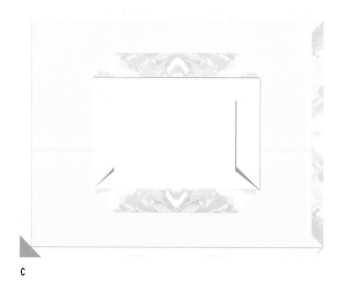

C

Creativity

• Personalize a frame with the subject's name. Decide on the dimensions of your finished frame and divide that into regular spaces. For example, with the name "Shaun," your frame could be 6 inches high with each letter-block unit 1 inch high. Fill each unit with a letter sized to fit. It looks graphically more interesting if the letters run down one side of the frame and the characters are all decorative capital letters.

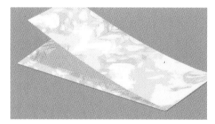

D

E

6. Mix a paint color that matches a predominating color in your paper. Paint the inner edge of all four corners on the inside of the frame, so that when the marbled paper is cut and turned under, none of the white Bristol board will show.

7. Place the marbled design for the front of your frame face down on your work surface and apply spray mount or a glue stick. Carefully center the Bristol board frame over this and adhere.

8. With the craft knife and straight-edge, cut a small box (approximately 2 x 3 inches) in the center of the marbled paper, leaving a margin of 1 inch to fold under. Cut diagonally into the four corners. Turn the four flaps under neatly, ensuring that no Bristol board shows on the right side. **(See Illustration C.)** Trim the outer four corners on the diagonal to create miters. Fold each of the four sides over the edges of the Bristol board, making sure that the corners are covered properly. Let dry.

9. Meanwhile, cover the other $7^1/_2$- x 10-inch piece of board the same way, omitting the step where you cut out the central portion. Let dry.

10. For the easel stand, cut a piece of the printed paper 5 x 8 inches and cover one side of the stand in the same manner. Let dry.

11. Cut a piece of printed paper $2^3/_4$ x $5^3/_4$ inches. Glue this to the other side of the easel stand, to cover it completely **(See Illustration D.)** Let dry. Score the easel stand at a horizontal spot 1 inch from the top and fold it slightly.

12. Glue the top 1-inch portion of the easel to the back panel of the frame, centered left to right. **(See Illustration E.)** The bottom edge of the stand should be $^1/_4$ inch above the bottom edge of the frame so it will lean properly. Let dry.

13. Place the front of the frame face down and run a thick line of glue from a glue gun around the bottom and two side edges, about $^1/_2$ inch in from the edge. You can also use white glue or double-sided tape.

14. Once everything is thoroughly dry, slip your photograph into the unglued slot at the top of the frame. To protect the photo you can also insert a thin sheet of acetate, available at art supply stores.

DESK ACCESSORIES

It's fun to personalize the objects on your desk. Consider using the logo you designed (see page 51) to make a businesslike set of accessories. The power of your computer may also suggest some other ideas. How about adorning these items with an abstract pattern that complements the furniture, wall art, or filing cabinets in your office?

The "try-as-you-go" technique we used to create our all-over design is loads of fun. Experiment to your heart's content, but be sure to save your work often so you can back out of effects you don't like. The only problem you're likely to encounter is selecting which of the many wild designs is your favorite. You can print on regular paper and adhere it with spray adhesive, or use self-adhesive paper, which not only saves a step but offers a choice of various colors as well as in different surface finishes from shiny to matte.

We show you how to make a pencil holder, a lidded box, an attractive portfolio for important—or unimportant—papers, and a desk blotter with special features. Combine these with the magazine file (page 122) and the furniture decoupage project (page 128) and you can coordinate your entire office!

(see page 51) ... (page 122) ... (page 128)

What You'll Need

MATERIALS
12-ounce smooth-sided tin can
High-quality paper, either self-adhesive or plain
Small cardboard file box (available in craft or art supply stores)
Foam board, two 9- x 12-inch pieces
1½-inch-wide library binding tape (available at some stationery stores, or the scrapbooking department of craft stores) or other decorative tape, 3 yards
Ribbon in coordinating color, 1 yard
Smooth-surface desk blotter

TOOLS
Craft knife
Self-healing cutting mat
Scissors
Masking tape
Small piece of scrap cloth
Spray adhesive (if using plain paper)
Spray polyurethane, decoupage glue, or other sealant
White acrylic paint
Small paintbrush
Disposable foam brush

ART
Clip art or self-created artwork

SOFTWARE
Image-editing program

SKILL LEVEL
Intermediate

COMPLETION TIME
Pencil cup: 1 hour
Box: 1 hour
Portfolio: 2½ hours
Blotter: 3 hours

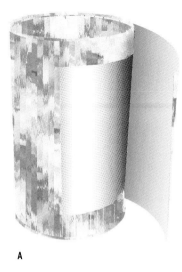

A

Creativity

• Cans and boxes come in so many shapes and sizes, and these techniques can easily be adapted to suit your project. Search out small boxes and pencil cups at craft stores.

• Think of other rooms that would benefit from good-looking coordinated items. Jazz up your kitchen or laundry room, cover boxes to hold your CDs, or make special mystery boxes for children.

• The design is the starting point: use patterns, words, and pictures for creativity. For an office, think about interesting ways to display the company logo. If you want to make a gift for a teacher, create a collage of images that relate to the person's special subject matter.

Pencil Cup

1. Create a design in your painting or drawing program. All-over patterns work best for this. As in the frame project (see pages 114–16), you can distort, alter, and apply effects to any image to create your design. We started with a spray of orange tones from our spray-paintbrush in a paint program, then dabbed on blotches of yellow with the small paintbrush tool. Next we used our special effects filter tools to swirl the colors together. Once we arrived at our all-over image for the cup we saved the design and several variations of it, which we used throughout this group of projects.

2. Measure your cup. (Ours measured 10 inches in circumference by 5 inches high.) You will be using this measurement to determine the sizes for four pieces: the outside, the inside, the top rim, and the bottom, as follows:
   • The length of the outside piece is the circumference plus a $1/2$-inch overlap, with a height $1/8$ inch less than the height of the can. (Our outside piece measured $10^1/2$ inches by $4^7/8$ inches.)
   • The inside piece will have the same length, and a height $1/8$ inch less than the outside piece (in our case, $10^1/2$ x $4^3/4$ inches).
   • The strip for the top rim is the same length again, by 2 inches wide.
   • For the bottom, you'll need a circle the diameter of the can plus 1 inch all around. Trace around the can to make a circle, then add the larger circle by tracing around a glass or saucer that is about an inch larger.

3. Determine how may sheets of paper you will need to accommodate these four pieces, and remember to take your printer margins into consideration. For our cylinder, three sheets were enough.

4. Print the needed pages. Allow to dry thoroughly.

5. Trim the four pieces to size. If you are using self-adhesive paper, peel the backing as you go. If you are using spray adhesive, position the pieces face down on a protected surface and spray lightly.

6. Apply the rim-covering strip to the inside top edge of the can, overlapping the ends. Using small sharp scissors, clip the paper at $1/2$-inch intervals on the outside edge and fold the edges down over the can rim. Smooth out and rub with a small piece of cloth to ensure adhesion. Apply the circle piece to the bottom of the can, clip the outer edge as before, and smooth the pieces up the side of the can with the cloth. Position the inside piece carefully and smooth it in place with the cloth. Wrap the outside piece over the surface of the can, smoothing as you go. **(See Illustration A.)** For added protection, spray with polyurethane or brush with decoupage glue or other sealant.

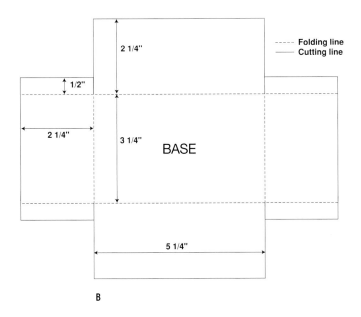

2 1/4"

1/2"

2 1/4"

3 1/4" BASE

5 1/4"

B

- - - - Folding line
——— Cutting line

- - - - Folding line
——— Cutting line

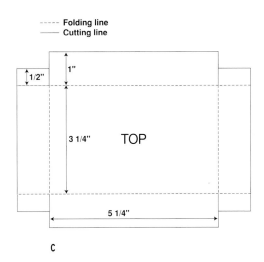

1/2" 1"

3 1/4" TOP

5 1/4"

C

Box

1. Paint the inside of the box and over the edges of the opening so that none of the original cardboard will show on completion.

2. Calculate how many sheets of printer paper will be needed to cover your box. For a recipe box that holds 3- x 5-inch index cards we printed two sheets, one for the top and one for the base. Apply our templates **(see Illustrations B and C)** to your layout using the image you created for the pencil cup. You may need to adapt our measurements to fit your box.

3. Print the requisite number of sheets and allow them to dry. Trim them along the solid outside lines.

4. If you are using self-adhesive paper, peel the backing as you go. If you are using spray adhesive, position the pieces face down on a protected surface and spray lightly. Proceed to wrap each piece around the box, starting with the bottom and working upward. **(See Illustration D.)** Smooth the pieces with a small piece of cloth to ensure adhesion. For added protection, spray with polyurethane or brush with decoupage glue or other sealant.

D

Portfolio

To create the portfolio we applied paper to both sides of foam board, then connected the two pieces with a binding to form a spine. Two pieces of ribbon allow you to tie the portfolio closed.

1. Print four sheets of paper with the design you created for the pencil cup. Allow to dry.

2. Cut two 9- x 12-inch pieces of foam board.

3. If you are using self-adhesive paper, peel the backing as you go. If you are using spray adhesive, position the pieces face down on a protected surface and spray lightly. Adhere one sheet of paper to each side of the two pieces of foam board. For added protection, spray with polyurethane or brush with decoupage glue or other sealant.

4. To form a binding that connects the two pieces, place them side by side and attach them to each other with library binding or decorative tape. **(See Illustration E.)** Shut the two pieces together like a book, with the tape on the inside. Tape over the exposed hinge on the outside, then encase the remaining edges with the library binding or decorative tape so no white edges show. **(See Illustration F.)** When applying the finishing tape along the two outer edges, insert a one-foot length of ribbon in the center of each side, at a right angle to portfolio edge, so the portfolio can be tied shut.

E

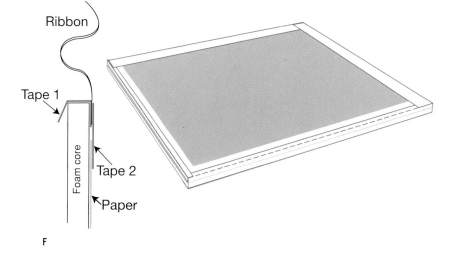

Ribbon

Tape 1

Foam core

Tape 2

Paper

F

Blotter

As desktops have changed, so have desk blotters. We found an interesting one at a business supply store that has a clear plastic overlay that can be written on with a dry-erase marker. We added some special features to our initial image (the all-over pattern) to create a coordinating covering for the blotter.

1. Measure your blotter and create a document of the appropriate size. We will be using the tiling feature (see page 33) to print this, so you may want to check your user's manual for more information. Lay out your elements—we centered a name plaque across the top, placed a linear calendar down one side, and added a notes space on the other side. Use decorative elements to dress it up. **(See Illustration G.)**

2. Tile this document on your printer. Carefully trim the margins with a craft knife and straightedge. Reassemble your original design, adhering the pieces to the blotter under the plastic cover with spray adhesive. Trim any paper that extends beyond the blotter.

Tip

Although self-adhesive paper seems like a natural choice for this project, it is tricky to use with tiled images, since very careful positioning is all-important and self-adhesive paper is not repositionable.

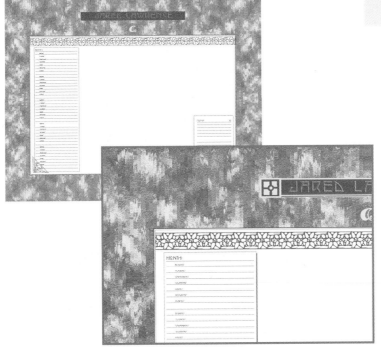

G

MAGAZINE FILE

This nice-looking technique actually strengthens the inexpensive cardboard files that you can buy in office supply houses and other stationery sources. The thin cardboard boxes are generally not very attractive, but with this project you can make a charming addition to any home or office.

What You'll Need

MATERIALS
Self-adhesive label paper
Fold-up cardboard magazine file

TOOLS
Craft knife
Self-healing cutting mat
Spray varnish or polyurethane

ART
Scanned images, clip art

SOFTWARE
Painting and page-layout
  programs

SKILL LEVEL
Easy

COMPLETION TIME
1½ hours

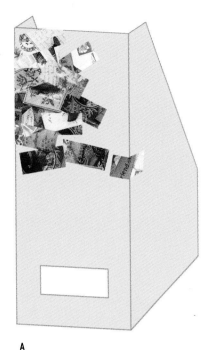

A

1. In an image-editing program, create a collage of all sorts of related motifs—handwritten letters, old photos, other memorabilia. Key the colors to one another to create a pleasing effect. Use sepia-toned pictures and objects for an old-fashioned feel, or bright colors for a modern office. We took one image at a time, erased the background, and placed it on one page. As each small picture was added, we moved it around on the page so that it slightly overlapped the other images and formed a harmonious combination. Look for variations in size and coloring.

2. Determine the amount of area to be covered. As a rough guide, plan on about six sheets per magazine file. Print six pages on the self-adhesive label paper. This paper is slightly more prone to smearing than plain bond paper, so allow each sheet to dry thoroughly—about ten minutes.

3. Trim off all the white edges that surround the central printable area of the labels. Apply the labels to the file randomly. **(See Illustration A.)** As you begin to cover more area, look for interesting image and color juxtapositions. At the corners and edges, cut labels to fit when the space or the design requires. Be sure all the labels are smoothly adhered.

4. Carefully spray the final surface with two coats of varnish or polyurethane. Allow to dry thoroughly between coats and after the final coat.

Creativity

• Antique-looking, romantic images will yield a soft look but don't forget the possibilities of bright graphics. Big block letters in circus colors will create an attractive merging of colors and shapes since the readability is broken up as you apply the individual labels.

• Vary the look by using different sizes of labels. Mailing labels will give you a less abstract look. Try using postcard-type pictures on larger self-adhesive labels to create a travel theme.

• Photographs also take on a look of their own when handled this way. And of course, if you're storing collections of magazines like *National Geographic*, Old World maps and old travel photos make an ideal choice for adorning the file box.

• Think about scanning some pages of the magazines themselves to create the images for the boxes—fashion magazines in a file covered with high-style photographs, or gardening magazines in files covered with floral shots.

MEMORY DRAWER

We got this idea after making one too many bulging memory books—too much stuff and not enough pages. We also had three-dimensional objects that didn't fit well into a book. Life is much easier if you can simply pop things into a nicely appointed drawer instead of painstakingly gluing them into book after book. We simply took over a whole drawer and made it a nostalgia trip. Isn't there an underutilized drawer in a spare bedroom that you could use? We already had all of our materials for future scrapbooking stuffed in one drawer of a guest bedroom that rarely got used, so we decided to transform it into a more organized approach to memorabilia. We lined the bottom of the drawer with wallpaper, then designed a coordinating border for the sides of the drawer. It was fun to create designs to complement the wallpaper pattern.

What You'll Need

MATERIALS
Drawer
Wallpaper or shelf-lining paper, enough to cover the bottom of the drawer
High-quality paper, either self-adhesive or plain
Foam board, two 30- x 40-inch sheets
½-wide ribbon, about ½ yard

TOOLS
Small scissors
Craft knife
Self-healing cutting mat
Ruler
White glue or double-sided tape
1-inch-wide transparent tape
Decoupage glue (if using plain paper)
Glue gun and glue sticks
Cellophane tape (optional)

ART
Computerized photographs, clip art, scanned images

SOFTWARE
Image-editing program

SKILL LEVEL
Advanced

COMPLETION TIME
4 to 6 hours

A

B

1. Cut a piece of wallpaper or shelf-lining paper large enough to cover the bottom of the drawer plus an extra inch all around. Line the draw with this paper, running the extra inch up the sides of the drawer. Secure the paper with glue or double-sided tape.

2. In your painting or image-editing software, create a design of flowers or other interesting motifs that coordinate with your wallpaper. We copied and pasted flower motifs from clip art and other sources onto a blank page. As we added each motif, we moved it around on the page so that it slightly overlapped other motifs. We also repeatedly copied some of the flowers and pasted them else-where in the composition, resizing some and rotating others in 90-degree and 180-degree increments to tie the design together visually. **(See Illustrations A and B.)**

3. Print enough copies to go around the inner sides of the drawer plus a little extra for positioning. Our drawer was 4 inches deep. To calculate how many pages we needed, we took the length of the drawer ($15^1/_4$ inches) times the width (18 inches) times two (four sides to a drawer). This number we divided by 7 inches (the approx-imate printable width of an $8^1/_2$- x 11-sheet of paper). We printed ten sheets.

4. Trim the sheets to the depth of the drawer and be sure to trim off any white margins. Starting at one corner, glue one sheet at a time to the inner side of the drawer using decoupage or white glue. Continue gluing sheets until all four sides of the drawer are covered. Allow the drawer to dry thoroughly. If the drawers were slightly uneven along the top edges, go back and neatly trim with a craft knife so they are flush with the top edge of the drawer.

Tip

Self-adhesive paper doesn't stick as well to wood as glue does, so it's best to use regular paper and glue for covering the drawer sides.

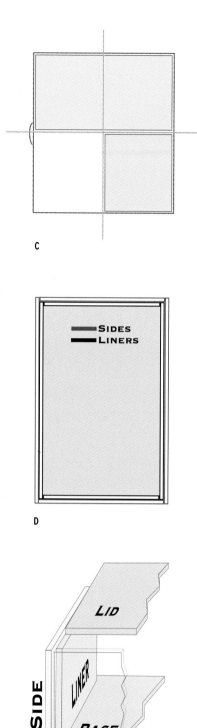

C

D

SIDES
LINERS

SIDE LID LINER BASE

E

5. Plan how to divide your drawer. An easy approach is to think of the drawer as divided into four quadrants. **(See Illustration C.)** (You may not actually make four partitions, but it helps to mentally divide the space into fourths.) We made one box that covers a little less than half the drawer ($^1/_4$ inch less in width and length than the space available), then made a second box that uses up just less than half the remaining space. The last quadrant can be kept open or can be further fitted with one or two more small boxes.

6. Determine the exact measurements for each box: the final height, width, and depth of each partitioned area. Use our measurements as a guideline, adjusting the dimensions to match your drawer. Be sure to give yourself enough ease to accommodate the lid by making the height of the lid supports at least $^1/_4$ inch less than the depth of the drawer. The following dimensions are based on our largest box.
 • The base piece equals the box length and width. Ours was $15^1/_4$ x $8^3/_4$ inches.
 • The two side pieces equal the exact length and depth of the box, minus the width of the foam board. These pieces sit on *top* of the base piece, so subtract that thickness from the measurement. Cut two more side pieces that are equal to the width and height of the box, minus the thickness of the foam board from *both* dimensions. Because our box was $15^1/_4$ inches long x $8^3/_4$ inches wide x $3^3/_4$ inches deep and our foam board was $^1/_8$ inch thick, we cut two side pieces each measuring $15^1/_4$ x $3^5/_8$ inches and two sides each measuring $8^1/_2$ x $3^5/_8$ inches.
 • The four "liner" pieces must fit snugly inside the box, forming the support for the lid. When the box is closed, the top of the lid should be flush with the box sides. The measurements for the liner pieces are the side dimensions minus the thickness of the board ($^1/_8$ inch) on both ends, and minus the thickness of the board from the depth to accommodate the lid. Since our longer side was $15^1/_4$ x $3^5/_8$ inches, we needed two liner pieces measuring $14^3/_4$ x $3^1/_2$ inches. For the shorter side, which measured $8^5/_8$ x $3^5/_8$ inches, our liner pieces were 8 x $3^1/_2$ inches.
 • The lid is the same dimension as the base piece minus the thickness of the foam board around each side. Since the base was $15^1/_4$ x $8^3/_4$ inches, we cut a lid measuring 15 x $8^1/_2$ inches.
 • Apply this same calculation method to your other box partitions and cut them out.

7. Using a glue gun or white glue, assemble the boxes. Place the base on a firm surface and glue each of the sides securely to the base and to each other. **(See Illustrations D and E.)** Be sure to position the sides *on* the base, not *beside* it. Reinforce the edges with tape if necessary. As you insert each liner piece, use a bit of glue to secure it to the side piece. When the glue has cooled or dried, tape over the outside seams for added strength.

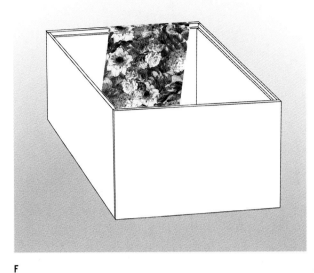

F

8. To cover the boxes, you can use the images you created before or compose new ones. The box designs may repeat, complement, or contrast with the drawer lining. To calculate the surface area required for the top and bottom, both inside and outside, multiply the length times the width (in our case, 15 x 8³/₄ = 131.25 square inches). Multiply this by four (two surfaces for the top, inside and outside, and two surfaces for the bottom, inside and outside; our figure was 525). Multiply these dimensions together and then multiply again by four (15 x 3³/₄ = 56.25 x 4 = 225). Multiply these two numbers together, then multiply again by four (8³/₄ x 3³/₄ = 32.81 x 4 = 131.25). Add these numbers together (525 + 225 + 131.25 = 881.25). Divide by 70, which is the approximate number of square inches per sheet of 8¹/₂- x 11-inch paper (881.25 ÷ 70 = 12.6). Thus we determined that we needed to print approximately thirteen sheets for that box.

9. Print enough sheets to cover all the boxes, inside and out. You can use regular paper if you want to glue it to the boxes, or self-adhesive paper if you'd like to skip the gluing process.

10. Cut the printed sheets into two or three pieces of approximately equal size. Adhere the pieces to the outside of the box as for decoupage, wrapping them onto the inside surface. Be careful to maintain the shelf for the lid. **(See Illustration F.)** Cover the entire box completely, then cover both sides of the lid. Save a few small printed pieces to use in step 12.

11. Spray two thin coats of varnish over the box, inside and out. Allow to dry thoroughly between applications and after the second coat.

12. Cut a 4-inch piece of ribbon and fold it in half. Glue it to the front underside of the lid so that the fold pokes up enough to grab onto when the lid is on. Adhere a small piece of printed paper over the raw edges of ribbon. Repeat for each lid.

Creativity

• You can use any theme for this project and organize the boxes in a different relationship. If the drawer is very deep, consider stacking some of the boxes. You may also want to use the computer to generate text or images that reflect what will be placed in each box.

• These lovely boxes don't have to be hidden away in drawers—make some as gifts. Create a special one for a going-away party and gather up all sorts of funny and sentimental oddments to remind the recipient of home. Send a box filled with goodies to a new mother. Tie the boxes with beautiful ribbons or decorate the covers with additional embellishments such as dried flowers or seashells.

DECOUPAGE TABLE

We took a small piece of furniture from a spare bedroom—with tired old paint and a very boring look—and turned it into a delightful signature piece. We have also created a whole suite of bedroom furniture from mismatched castoffs using this technique. It takes some work and time but it is worth every minute of the effort.

Select furniture with mostly flat surfaces, since the paper must be glued on and it can be tricky to cover intricate curves. Choose a theme for your images. We used fabric samples from old Japanese obis (the sash worn around the kimono)—their rich patterns and textures were perfect. Consider using scans from the draperies, sheets, or quilt that may already be in the room where the furniture will be placed. Pick three or four fabric swatches or other images as a starting point. As you manipulate the images, you will begin to expand your horizons: resize one picture, cut out a detail from another, change the color of a particular element. Imagine how the images will complement the style and size of the piece and adjust your composition accordingly.

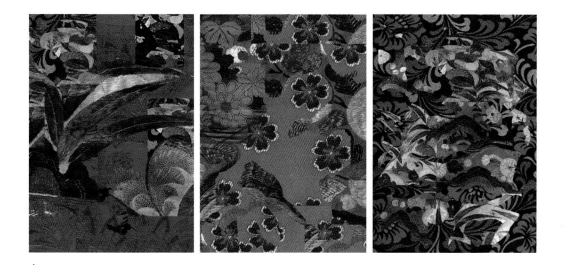

A

1. Scan each swatch or other image source. In an image-editing program, retouch any wrinkles in the fabric, adjust colors and sizing, and remove any unwanted details. Save each source image as a separate file, named either with letters, numbers, or the type of image. They should all be saved in the same format and at the same resolution so that you can combine them.

2. Open a new document. Open up one of the swatches, and copy and paste it into the new document. Create a new layer and repeat this process, using the second fabric swatch. Create four layers, each with a different swatch on it. In the top layer, use an eraser tool to selectively remove sections of the image. The swatch just below it will appear. If you make a mistake, simply revert, or undo the action. If the fabric has a motif on a white ground, you can use the magic wand tool, select the white area, and erase it all in

one fell swoop. Repeat the process for the second layer, removing portions so that the next lower surfaces will appear.

3. Keep checking your work by displaying all four layers. Make sure you don't remove all the images from one area on all four levels, leaving a hole in your pattern. If this does happen, you can fix it by using the lasso tool to select an area, copy it, and move it to cover the hole. Mix up the motifs so they don't repeat in a discernible pattern, and let the patterns seem to flow into each other.

4. When you are satisfied with the look of your new design, condense the file into one layer and save the patterns you created. **(See Illustration A for examples of our patterns.)**

5. Make five variations, revealing more of one image and less of another, or omitting one altogether, making them as visually rich as possible.

(continued on next page)

Creativity

• Create a design around some important event: commemorate a wedding, anniversary, or other milestone.

• Send someone off to college with a unique bookcase, perhaps adorned with images from childhood.

• Victorian ephemera is a perfect subject for this technique. By using computer printouts of the images, you can keep the originals! Look for copyright-free clip art books that you can scan, rearrange, recolor, and resize.

• For a child's room, make it a learning experience! Put letters of the alphabet on dresser drawers or a small table.

B

6. Once your image composition is complete, calculate the surface area of your furniture. First, measure the largest flat areas and approximate smaller areas such as legs or railings. Then calculate surface area using the standard formula of multiplying length times width. This will give you the approximate number of square inches in your furniture piece.

7. Since your printer will not print a full $8\frac{1}{2}$- x 11-inch page, calculate your yield per page by figuring out the dimensions of the printable area of your sheet. (For example, our printable area of $7\frac{1}{2}$ x 10 inches yields approximately 70 square inches total).

8. Divide the square inches of your furniture by the figure you arrived at in step 7 to find out the number of pages needed. (Our small table, which measured approximately 1200 square inches, took less than 20 sheets.)

9. Print the necessary number of pages, plus 10 percent more to allow for cutting, overlapping, and matching or mismatching to get the right look. Trim off the white borders.

10. Wash the piece of furniture with warm water and a soft cloth to clean off any dust or oils. If the surface is very glossy, rough it up with a light sanding.

11. Experiment with general planning before you glue on any pieces. Play around with some of the printouts, arranging them, cutting them into smaller pieces, and plotting out how you will handle corners and other odd shapes. We found that cutting a sheet in half lengthwise made a good strip to wind around a leg. Prefold any places that must wrap around edges. (This helps in positioning and will also help the piece to adhere.) When you have completed your planning, you'll be ready to glue. Be sure to start in an inconspicuous spot so early mistakes don't show; from there you'll move to the hard-to-reach areas, saving the easiest parts for last.

12. Place your first section face down on a page of an old phone book or newspaper, brush glue over the entire surface, and place it on the furniture. Carefully smooth out any air bubbles or wrinkles. Brush another coat of glue over the glued-on pieces to seal them. **(See Illustration B.)** As you continue brushing glue on subsequent pieces, keep moving to a clean page of the phone book or a new area of newspaper. When a full sheet will not fit, position the piece without glue, mark it lightly with a pencil, and trim it to size. As you proceed to cover the entire piece of furniture, keep an eye on the overall design. Allow the completed piece to dry overnight.

13. Cover the entire piece of furniture with three coats of polyurethane, sanding lightly between coats.

14. Since there will be some slight irregularities in the surface, put a piece of glass over the top if you are going to use it for a writing surface. You may also want to use glass if the furniture may be subjected to liquid, such as a coffee table on which drinks may be placed.

WALLPAPER DECALS

When you would like a quick and easy pick-me-up for any room, here is a fun project that takes very little time and is as permanent or as temporary as you wish. Each motif is isolated and printed on self-adhesive paper. We output a bunch of them and attached them to the bathroom walls. This project is so easy that the toughest part of the job is picking the beautiful images you would like to use!

You can use a digital camera, as we did here to capture hydrangeas in bloom. (This design complements the wallpaper on page 136.) Or look for great photographs in copyright-free digital art collections or other sources.

What You'll Need

MATERIALS
Self-adhesive paper

TOOLS
Small scissors
Decorative-edge scissors (optional)
Brush-on polyurethane (optional)
Disposable brush (optional)

ART
Scanned objects, computerized
   photographs, clip art

SOFTWARE
Image-editing program

SKILL LEVEL
Easy

COMPLETION TIME
1 hour

1. Scan your images. Open the photos in an image-editing program and save each design as an isolated image under a different title. Isolate desired areas by erasing all of the background. **(See Illustrations A and B.)** Correct the color, remove unwanted parts, and clean up any other imperfections. If you are combining more than one image, make sure that each is sized proportionally, in the same format and at the same ppi.

(continued on next page)

A

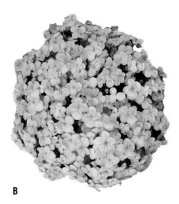

B

- Any object that can be printed on a sheet can be used. Scatter pictures of family and friends around a room, or use large letters to spell out names or an inspirational quote.

- Self-adhesive papers come in many colors, so experiment with different backgrounds to add richness to a design.

You may want to print drafts of the pieces and tape them gently to the wall to test the eye appeal of the design and to help plan your layout.

2. Open a new document for the final image. Open one of the isolated motifs (in our case, a scan of leaves), and copy and paste it to this blank page. Open the second image (the hydrangea), and copy and paste it to the page. Arrange the composition so the images overlap slightly. Resize as necessary; you want the image to fill as much of the printable page area as possible. (Depending on your design, you may be able to fit two decals on one page.)

3. If desired, fill the background with a shade to blend with your wall color to avoid having to cut exactly around the outline of the image. We chose a mottled tone. **(See Illustration C.)** Save this finished design in the format and at the resolution best suited to your hardware and software.

4. Print the required number of images. Let them rest for at least half an hour to allow the ink to dry thoroughly.

5. Cut out your motifs. You may also consider using decorative-edge scissors instead of regular scissors.

6. If your design requires a very accurate placement, you may want to lightly mark the position with a pencil.

7. Until you become comfortable positioning the decals, start in the least visible area of the room so that early mistakes are less noticeable. (Behind a door is generally a good choice.) Peel off the backing paper and smooth the images onto the wall. We put ours up in a random pattern, so precision wasn't necessary.

8. To make the decals more permanent—especially in a bathroom, where they will be subject to frequent moisture—brush on polyurethane and allow to dry.

C

WALLPAPER BORDER

Slightly more involved than the previous project, this is another approach to adding color and patterns to your walls. This variation is based on a combination of photographs, taken with a digital camera, from which we created a beautiful and realistic wallpaper frieze. For a kitchen, try photographing a collection of teacups as we did, or capture a pretty group of plates.

The idea is to transform some quick photos into something wonderful. Since digital cameras allow you to see the results immediately, you can experiment with lighting and arrangements until you are quite happy with the results. A second benefit of a digital camera is that you don't have to waste film, money, or processing time to get results worthy of a professional. If you don't have a digital camera, use scanned objects, photographs, or some clip art that you love.

What You'll Need

MATERIALS
Plain bond or photo-quality paper, legal size

TOOLS
Craft knife or rotary cutter
Straightedge
Self-healing cutting mat
Old phone book or lots of old newspaper
White glue, decoupage glue, or rubber cement
Brush-on polyurethane
Disposable brushes
Wallpaper smoother (available in paint and hardware stores)

ART
Computerized photographs, clip art

SOFTWARE
Image-editing program

SKILL LEVEL
Easy

COMPLETION TIME
1½ hours

1. Take photographs of a collection of items: plates, cups, bottle caps, matchbook covers, or whatever you collect. Also photograph a shelf that they will appear to sit on, if appropriate to your intended design. If you don't have a collection of objects, find appropriate images in your clip art collections. We shot pictures of a several cups and saucers and then shot a picture of a shelf for the cups to sit on. Take all the photographs from the same angle and with the same light so your images will look more consistent and you will save time in image editing.

2. If you used a film camera, scan the processed prints. Clean up the images by correcting the color, removing unwanted parts, and isolating the selected motif in each photograph. Erase all of the background, leaving just the motif itself, and save each of these "knocked-out" images with a different title but at the same resolution. Be sure to resize each image so they will all be approximately the same size when combined.

(continued on next page)

3. Create a blank horizontal page, 14 inches wide x 8¹/₂ inches high. Open the image of the shelf, then copy and paste it onto this blank page. Open the image of the first object, and copy and paste it onto the horizontal page. Arrange the object so that it seems to sit on the shelf. **(See Illustration A.)** Continue to open object images, copying and pasting them into your horizontal page. Overlap the ends of the shelf to form a continuous border and continue filling the shelf with your chosen objects. Resize as necessary if any of the images are out of proportion with one another.

4. Adjust the background color. Choose a solid shade to match your wall color or create a subtle pattern to complement your room decor.

5. When your page is full, crop the image so the edges are straight on both sides. This will make for a smooth join when you paste the border to the wall. Copy and paste this image on the same page so you will have two lengths on one page. **(See Illustration B.)** Save this in the format and at the resolution best suited to your hardware and software.

6. Check your printer specifications to be sure exactly how much printable page length you have. Your figure should be about 13¹/₂ inches; if it is substantially different, use your own measurement in the upcoming calculation. Next, determine your wall space by measuring the distance around each wall, subtracting for doors or windows that will not be covered. Divide this perimeter measurement by 13¹/₂ inches and add 15 percent for positioning, overlapping, and other adjustments. This will give you the number of pages you need. For instance, our room perimeter measured 240 inches and when we divided by 13¹/₂ we got 18 lengths. After adding 15 percent, we determined that we needed 21 sheets.

A

B

7. Print the required number of sheets on plain bond or photo-quality paper. Let them rest for at least half an hour. Once they are thoroughly dry, trim away the margins with a straightedge and a craft knife or rotary cutter.

8. Before you paste any borders into place, plan their positioning by laying out the sheets on the floor around the room. You may want to emphasize an area by adding cut-out motifs, or use your extra print-outs to avoid a repetition. As you put up your border you may want to cut out sections of one border to add variety and interest to the overall look.

9. When you are satisfied that the overall effect is balanced and pleasing, proceed with hanging the borders. Place your first sheet face down on a page of an old phone book or newspaper, brush glue over the entire surface, and press it carefully onto the wall, using the wallpaper smoother to ease out any wrinkles or bubbles and ensure a good bond. Start in the least conspicuous corner of the room—this gives you a chance to get used to handling the paper and the glue; it also makes any irregular pattern matching less obvious in case your motifs don't match up exactly when you get all the way around the room and back to where you started. Continue to paste sheets on the wall, either butting them together or overlapping very slightly. As you continue brushing glue on subsequent pieces, keep moving to a clean page of the phone book or a new area of newspaper.

10. As you complete each section of wall, step back and check it from a distance. If something needs changing, you can reposition or add more motifs at this point. When you are satisfied with the whole border, examine it carefully to make sure all the ends are pasted down firmly and there are no wrinkles. Let the border dry for about 12 hours.

11. The border should be sealed since the inks may run if splashed with liquids. Seal the entire border with a thin coat of polyurethane or decoupage glue. Polyurethane may require a second coat.

Creativity

• Run a favorite quote in a fancy typeface around a family room. Or create a border of family photos or favorite animals to run around a child's bedroom. Just remember that since a child's eye level is much lower than an adult's, it's generally better to hang the border midway or two-thirds of the way up the wall, rather than at the very top.

• For a den or library, design a border of books on a shelf. To camouflage a closet door, stack the borders one on top of another to create a faux bookshelf.

• For a more elaborate finished edge, instead of trimming the margins with a straightedge, use decorative-edge scissors or a scalloped rotary cutter blade.

• The border technique is very effective on a floor. Make sure to seal a floor border very thoroughly with at least five or six coats of polyurethane, since floors get much more wear and tear than walls. Try adorning the four outer edges of a floor with flowers that match the room's decor.

WALLPAPER

Here is a very interesting technique for using computer printouts to make unique wallpaper for any room in the house. We created a surround for a bathroom tub area. We stopped short of the ceiling, but you could conceivably cover all four walls, the ceiling, and even the floor if you wish! In one of our projects we completely covered the walls and ceilings of a small guest room—it's fun to be so bold with modern technology. Pick a theme and gather your resources to fit. Before you go wallpapering the whole house, though, you might want to try this out on one wall or in a little spare bedroom or pantry.

We used floral images from photographs taken in our garden. Other good sources are clip art books or old wallpaper sample books whose copyrights have expired. Look for complete, well-detailed pictures and keep your color scheme in mind, although you can modify the image tones to make sure the colors complement your room.

What You'll Need

MATERIALS
Plain bond paper, legal size

TOOLS
Scissors
Craft knife or rotary cutter
Straightedge
Self-healing cutting mat
Decorative-edge scissors
    (optional)
Old phone book or lots of old
    newspaper
White glue, decoupage glue,
    or rubber cement
Low-tack tape
Spray- or brush-on polyurethane
Disposable brushes
Wallpaper smoother (available
    in paint and hardware stores)

ART
Computerized photographs,
    clip art

SOFTWARE
Image-editing program

SKILL LEVEL
Advanced

COMPLETION TIME
6 to 12 hours

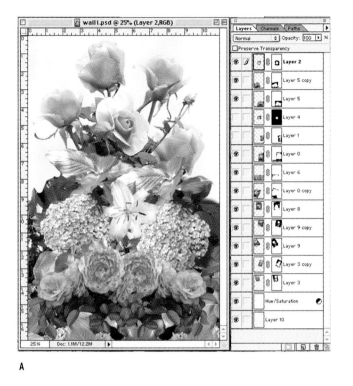

A

1. Scan your images at approximately 120–150 ppi. Correct the color, remove unwanted parts, and isolate the motifs you want to work with. (Remember, you don't have to clean up the images if you feel that their imperfections and age lend charm, but you may want to adjust the tones to match the colors to your room's decor.) Save all the images at the same resolution and resize each image so that it will be approximately the same size as all the other images you will be using.

2. Knock out the individual motifs that you want to work with by erasing all of the background and leaving just the irregular outlines of the object. Name and save each motif.

3. For the upper edge of the wallpaper, create a blank portrait-oriented page. Open a scan, and copy and paste it to this blank page. Open and paste any other images you will be using. Arrange them so they overlap slightly. Resize as necessary. Continue to open images, copying and pasting them into your page until you are happy with the image. We chose an irregular upper edge, rather than running the design all the way up the wall. **(See Illustration A.)** Save this in the format that is best suited to your hardware and software.

4. Make a second design that will be used as an overall pattern in the middle of the wall. Color-coordinate it with the primary design and keep an eye on proportions.

(continued on next page)

Tip

• You may want to print drafts of the designs and tape them to the wall with low-tack tape to test their eye appeal.

• If your printer has continuous-form paper-handling capability, make the image as long as your printer and editing software allow, usually around 44 inches. If you have made variations on each pattern, print a few extra sheets, since you may want to intersperse the sections with alternate images to add interest to the overall look.

B

5. Create a third document for the bottom of each wall and proceed as before. Be sure the three panels work well together. **(See Illustration B.)**

6. Calculate how much wall space you will be covering by measuring the width and height of each wall area to be papered. Multiply these two figures to arrive at the square footage, then subtract the area of doors or other openings that will not be covered. Since the complete wallpaper design is composed of three rows, each row is one-third of the total; therefore you will need to divide your total coverage area by 3 to determine the square footage for each row's design.

7. Check your printer specifications to be sure exactly how much printable page area you have. We used tabloid-sized paper (only some inkjet printers can accommodate this size paper; check your printer specifications), so each 11- x 17-inch sheet yielded about 187 square inches or about $1^1/_4$ square feet. For legal-size paper, divide your wall's square footage by .7 and add 15 percent for positioning, overlapping, and other adjustments. This conservative measurement will give you the number of pages you need to print. If you are using letter-size paper, you will have approximately $1^1/_2$ square feet per page.

8. Print the necessary number of sheets. Let them rest for at least half an hour.

9. Once the sheets are thoroughly dry, trim away the side and upper margins with a straightedge and a craft knife or rotary cutter. Trim the lower edge unevenly with scissors to help disguise the line where the layers will overlap. You may prefer to use decorative-edge scissors instead of regular scissors. If the design warrants it, trim close to the irregular shape of the outline in the top panel.

10. Tack one group of the top row panels together with low-tack tape and trim the background away from the motifs with scissors. Mark lightly on the back the order of the panels (1-2-3-4). Place them on the wall in that order and the cuts will match. **(See Illustration C.)**

c

11. Before you paste any of the sheets into place, plan their positioning. You may want to emphasize an area by adding cut-out motifs, or use extra printouts to avoid a repetition. Lay out the sheets on the floor around the room and check for positioning. When you are satisfied that the overall effect is balanced and pleasing, proceed.

12. Place the first sheet face down on a page of an old phone book or newspaper, brush glue over the entire surface, and press it carefully onto the wall, using the wallpaper smoother to ease out any wrinkles or bubbles and ensure a good bond. Start in the least conspicuous corner of the room—this gives you a chance to get used to handling the panels and the glue; it also makes any irregular pattern matching less obvious in case your motifs don't match up exactly when you get all the way around the room and back to where you started. Continue pasting images on the wall, overlapping slightly so the design is pleasing to the eye. We started with the bottom row, overlapped the bottom edge of the second row at the top of the bottom row,

then overlapped the third row the same way. As you continue brushing glue on subsequent pieces, keep moving to a clean page of the phone book or a new area of newspaper.

13. After you have completed each section of wall, step back and check it from a distance. If something needs changing, you can reposition or add more motifs at this point. We added a little pond to ours! We also could have cut out one or two small flowers and attach them on the overlaps or let them drift around the wall as if they were falling from the design.

14. Examine the edges and make sure all the pieces are pasted down firmly. Let the finished wall dry for about 12 hours.

15. The wallpaper must be sealed. Coat the entire wall with a thin layer of decoupage glue or polyurethane (either the spray-on or brush-on type). If you've hung the wallpaper in an area subject to a lot of moisture, such as the bathroom, choose the polyurethane, and apply a second coat when the first one is dry.

Creativity

• To add even more interest to the wall, make several variations of the designs, saving each one as a separate document. You could flip the whole image on its horizontal axis, then replace some of the motifs with others. Change the color of some of the motifs using your selection tools. Make copies of one of the motifs and resize it and add it to another version.

• Go for an antique look with images of old musical scores and old instruments. Tint the polyurethane with a stain for a romantic, aged look. If your images are black and white, change the black to another color like a deep blue or a sepiatone for a more subtle look.

RESOURCES

Much of what is called for in the projects is readily available, but there are some specialized materials, tools, and resources of which you will want to be aware. Also note that many craft-source Web sites feature project ideas and instructions.

Craft Supplies

Aleene's Creative Living
(800) 825-3363
www.aleenes.com
Extensive selection of all types of craft supplies. Check out the BoxMaker, a handy tool that helps make gift boxes from cover-weight paper.

BagWorks
(817) 446-8080
www.bagworks.com
Canvas products, including totes, vests, aprons, pillows, and window treatments; great for T-shirt transfer process.

Creative Paper Collections
(323) 965-2581
More than 180 specialty papers, card stock, and greeting cards, most with matching envelopes; many compatible with inkjet printers.

CTI Paper
(800) 284-7272 (call for retail locations)
www.thepapermill.com
Great papers for the craft industry.

Daige
(800) 645-3323
www.daige.com
Mounting and laminating products, including Rollataq, a permanent adhesive system that doesn't require sprays or dry mount supplies; comes in three desktop sizes (12, 24, and 36 inches) and a hand-held model.

Daniel Smith
(800) 426-6740
One of the best catalogs of artist's materials, including their exclusive iridescent watercolors. Great products and professional, helpful staff.

Dick Blick Art Materials
(800) 933-2542
www.dickblick.com
Mail-order art supplies catalog.

Hygloss Products
(800) 444-9456 (call for retail locations)
Quality arts and crafts papers, including velour paper, which will feed through most ink-jet printers.

Light Impressions
(800) 828-6216
Archival supplies: library binding tape, glues, boxes, pH-neutral products, more. Their "Tech Corner" offers information and tips.

Midwest Products Company
(219) 942-1134 (call for retail locations)
www.midwestproducts.com
Quality wood products for crafting; great for the T-shirt transfer process.

Nasco Arts & Crafts
(800) 558-9595
www.homeschool-nasco.com
Great source for schools and institutions.

Paper Access
(800) PAPER-01
Specialty papers for the crafter.

Paper Direct
(800) 272-7377
Specialty papers with preprinted designs, in a variety of colors.

Paper Patch
(801) 253-3018 (call for retail locations)
(800) 397-2737 (orders)
Acid-free printed background papers and other specialty printed papers.

Paper Showcase
(800) 287-8163
Papers for computer printers.
www.worldseasiest.com

Pearl Paint Company
(800) 451-PEARL
www1.viaweb.com/pearl/
A great source for all things artistic (fine arts, crafts, frames, and more), now with several stores in major cities across the U.S.

Phoenecian Papers
(800) 875-1500
Handmade, wood-free, recycled papers and envelopes, including beautiful papers with flower petals worked into the paper; sets of cards and envelopes; and bulk papers and folders.

Plickety Plunk Press
(805) 867-7007
www.plickityplunk.com
Tools and techniques of bookbinding: "Bookmaaker' kit and other fine bookbinding materials, kits, and supplies; also bone folders.

Print Paks
(503) 417-4926
www.printpaks.com
Super Jewelry Kit comes packed with all the supplies needed to make funky earrings, cool necklaces, beaded bracelets, and wildly colorful pins. You can easily convert your favorite photo into a beautiful jewelry.

PromoGraphics International
(954) 797-9600
www.freecolor.com
Digital printing on T-shirts, caps, mousepads, canvas bags, and other items.

Quill Corporation
(800) 789-6640
www.quillcorp.com
High-quality full-color papers that work in laser printers, ink-jet printers, and copiers. Free catalog and samples.

Saro Trading Company
(800) 662-7276
www.saro.com/
Fabrics that can be used in the T-shirt transfer process to make romantic and beautiful projects; linen napkins, Battenberg lace, and other items of very high quality.

Sax Arts & Crafts Catalog
(800) 558-6696
www.saxarts.com

Sunshine Discount Crafts
(800) 432-7455
www.sunshinecrafts.com

Xyron, Inc.
www.xyron.com
Their handy desktop laminator is fun and very versatile.

Hardware and Software

Adobe Systems Incorporated
(800) 272-3623
(206) 470-7693
(206) 470-7106
www.adobe.com
Adobe magazine, a valuable source for design ideas and technical help, is offered to all registered users of its products, including Pagemaker, Photoshop, Illustrator, and Persuasion.

Club Mac
(800) 258-2622
Mail-order source for Apple Macintosh supplies.

Chroma Graphics
(650) 375-1100
www.chromagraphics.com
Software tools for Photoshop: selecting objects, blending or changing colors.

DesignOnline
(815) 777-6365
www.dol.com
An online service for computer-based artists; its forums and content can be found on the net.

DTP Direct
(800) 395-7778
www.dtpdirect.com
A mail-order source with a graphics twist.

Dynamic Graphics
(800) 255-8800
(800) 488-3492
www.dgi.com
"Clipper,". monthly service for clip art in electronic and paper format in TIFF and EPS images with a monthly how-to magazine and training on CD-ROM. Great magazine, *Dynamic Graphics,* for small office/home office desktop projects and information. *Electronic Design,* aimed at the graphics professional, shows specific projects and techniques.

Educorp Direct
CD-ROMs and diskettes with software, shareware, and games.
(914) 347-2464
www.educorp.com

Epson
www.epson.com
Wide variety of ink-jet printers.

EyeWire
(800) 661-9410
www.eyewire.com
Innovative stock photographs, software, clip art, and fonts. Check out the "Tips and Tricks" sections in their catalog.

FontHaus
(800) 942-9110
www.fonthaus.com

Fonts Online
www.fontsonline.com

The Font Pool
www.fontpool.com
Resources for learning.

The Font Site
www.fontsite.com

Hewlett-Packard Company
Premier provider of scanners, computers, printers, supplies, and services.
www.hp.com

Lexmark International
www.lexmark.com
A well-recognized name in personal printers.

The Mac/PC Zone
(800) 248-0800
www.zones.com
Mail-order source for computers and supplies, both Macintosh and Intel-based.

Publisher's Toolbox
(800) 390-0461 (orders)
www.pubtool.com
Desktop publishing and graphics-related products.

Webopaedia.com
Specific answers to questions about technical terms, with references to products, other sites, and interesting information.
www.webopaedia.com

Publications

Creating Keepsakes Scrapbook Magazine
(801) 224-8235
www.creatingkeepsakes.com
Interesting family-oriented scrapbooking projects; crisp, clean graphics and easy-to-follow instructions.

HOW Magazine
(800) 333-1115
Creative and business issues, practical information, and inspiring works in the design field.

Hungry Minds Books
www.hungryminds.com
World-leading media, research, and publishing company.

I Love Remembering Magazine (D.O.T.S. Company)
(800) 965-0924
www.iloveremembering.com
Quarterly idea book showcasing the art of scrapbooking; lots of ideas for paper crafters.

Somerset Studio
(949) 380-7318
Wonderful magazine showcasing paper arts. Send in one of your creations—they run readers' works every month!

INDEX

Metric Conversion Table

MEASUREMENT	METRIC EQUIVALENT	
1/16 inch	0.16 cm	To convert inches to centimeters, multiply the inch measurement by 2.54. To convert yards to meters, multiply the yard measurement by 0.3048.
1/8 inch	0.32 cm	
1/4 inch	0.64 cm	
3/8 inch	1 cm	
1/2 inch	1.27 cm	
5/8 inch	1.59	
3/4 inch	1.91	
7/8 inch	2.22 cm	
1 inch	2.54 cm	
1 yard	91.44 cm (0.91 m)	